DATE DUE

THE ART OF
GROUP CONVERSATION

**A new breakthrough
in social communication**

RACHEL DAVIS DUBOIS ▶

MEW-SOONG LI ▶

ASSOCIATION PRESS

NEW YORK

THE ART OF

GROUP

CONVERSATION

A new breakthrough
in social communication

CONTENTS

FOREWORD

Democracy is something we all love—and something we take for granted. But, like everything else we love, democracy requires cultivation; otherwise we lose it. "Group conversation" is a technique for cultivating democracy afresh day by day—in a wide variety of social situations. As a technique it is simple. It has the simplicity of genius.

The authors of this book, experienced developers of the technique, define group conversation as "a way of helping a roomful of people, even strangers of mixed backgrounds, feel something of the warmth and trust of longtime friends and neighbors." I myself have marked the rapid success of the method in producing precisely this feeling of warmth and trust in an ethnically mixed group within the space of a brief hour, every minute of which was enjoyable. The process is effortless and playful, spontaneous and mirthful—in short, it is fun.

A session of group conversation is something good in its own right, like a game, like any wholesome relaxation; but its value reaches much further. It can be used as a prelude to an effective conference, to a serious group discussion, to achieving neighborhood co-operation, to the forming of interracial councils, or even to a subsequent series of group-therapy sessions—all depending upon the purpose of the initial gathering and the interests of the participants.

The technique is, of course, variable. With a mixed group, meeting for the first time, the element of play is stressed. With more homogeneous groups (such as those found in churches or clubs), the method allows for a more serious but equally friendly approach to the discussion of common problems.

To what is the success of this method due? I believe it is due to its skillful use of basic psychology. All of us like to regress occasionally to our childhood and to tell of some cherished memories of locations, of holidays, of games, duties, or customs that we know. Group conversation invites us to do so. All of us like to shuck off the burden of self-conscious reticence, and here we can do so in an atmosphere of play and acceptance. We have a longing to be taken for what we are (whatever our racial or regional background); we want the security that comes from telling of our own cultures; we want to share the common coin of our humanity with others. Further, we like food, holidays, folk songs, and dances. Group conversation may give expression to these interests, and in so doing strengthen our solidarity with others.

Layers of self-consciousness are peeled off, but with no violation of our privacy.

To my mind the most interesting psychological feature of the process is the swift way in which the participation of each individual in the group is elicited. He tells his name and where he is from. This initial participation makes it easier for him soon to recount his childhood and cultural memories. Before he knows it he may be demonstrating how he played marbles as a child, how a favorite song sounded, what a dance was like. And the whole group may soon become involved in a lively and co-operative performance with him. The participant does not *think* himself into a democratic way of acting (as lecturers, preachers, writers ask us to do), but rather *acts* himself into a democratic way of thinking. This is sound psychology.

The process seems so natural, and we have such a good time, that we do not realize that we have been guided by a technique of democracy; but it *is* a technique, a skill that group leaders can learn. This guidebook gives the results of rich and prolonged experiences, based upon hundreds of experiments. It shows what pitfalls to avoid, how to keep the group moving to its destination of mutual trust and enjoyment. It presents in full the logic of the case for group conversation as a tool for advancing world democracy and brotherhood.

GORDON W. ALLPORT
Harvard University

PREFACE

Do situations like these have a familiar ring?

- The board meeting has bogged down because everyone is too occupied defending his own point of view to listen to the next person. The impasse reflects the mood running through the organization because the proposed change in personnel policy has sharply divided the staff into two camps with seriously emotional overtones.
- Parents are frustrated because they cannot reach their teen-age children. Their noisy rock-and-rolling and midnight hot-rodding seem to be a rejection of the values on which they had been brought up.
- The people called to discuss an issue currently dividing the community represent a broad cross section, but there is little real participation in the discussion. There is a feeling of strangeness, even distrust, in the group, and the conference must get off to a quick good start.
- Parents and teachers in a newly integrated school avoid getting at the problems that are really bothering the youngsters and are less than frank about their

13

own feelings. An undercurrent of unrest and of unspoken hostility ensues.

* The guests invited to the Brotherhood church supper happily include visitors from the Negro congregation across town, a neighboring synagogue, a number of students from Cambodia, Turkey, Spain, Jamaica, Pakistan, and Indonesia. How break through the formality of introductions and the feeling of strangeness, and make each person feel truly welcome?

The Art of Group Conversation deals with problems such as these—problems which most democratic groups face at one time or another. Basically, they are problems of communication, the kind of difficulties that imply a need for faith—faith in one's self, faith in the next person, faith in the group.

What is needed is a kind of breakthrough, a reaffirmation of trust, a reconciliation with one's self, with each other, but even more with the unending possibilities for human growth and achievement which come with free, creative encounter.

This means that in our interrelationships, we must be sure that unconscious motivations do not get in the way of our words, that words do not get in the way of our feelings, and that feelings of fear and strangeness, of hostility and prejudice do not get in the way of free thoughtful exchange. Only then can we arrive at the kind of constructive decision and commitment that can be translated into productive action.

This book describes group conversation, a social

invention, an art form, which seeks to make this kind of breakthrough possible. If you work professionally with groups, or if you are one of the thirty million volunteer leaders who give of their time, energy, and talent to help make our democracy work, you will know how vital a feeling of acceptance can be, and you will want to become familiar with a process or technique that can create it. It can help all of us to understand and believe in our real and deeper selves, and to communicate more freely with each other. We offer this book because we believe that group conversation can help to release spiritual and creative forces which give meaning to life. It can bring to a group new directions and new perspective.

Actually, this book is written by the hundreds and hundreds of group conversations that we have conducted over many years, and by the thousands of people who have taken part in them, in many parts of the United States and in several other countries of the world. These sessions have enjoyed the sponsorship of groups that run the gamut from primary family units to private and semiprivate agencies, to civic and community organizations, public institutions, and our government's State Department. They have been carried out under the direction and aegis of the Workshop for Cultural Democracy, a pioneer organization in human relations and intercultural education, which has its headquarters in New York City. We acknowledge the important role of the organization in making this book possible. We are grateful also to the Lucius N. Littauer Foundation for its generous grant toward the typing of the manuscript.

Our new age of orbiting satellites, extraplanetary broadcast networks and vastly increased contacts between our country and the many peoples of the world, mean new challenges and new perspectives. They also mean more intricate economic and political arrangements and more complicated and confounding social problems. What is indicated is the need to reaffirm our belief in the true democratic tenets, those which can bring about the kind of renewal and reconciliation that will put to full use our rich human resources of race, creed, and ethnic backgrounds. Only through full, free communication can we transcend the barriers of distrust, hate, and bigotry that obtain when we cannot get through to one another.

Always must we be looking for ways to build those bridges over which heart can reach out to human heart in fellowship and trust.

Rachel Davis DuBois

Mew-soong Li

New York

THE ART OF
GROUP CONVERSATION

**A new breakthrough
in social communication**

1 : WHAT IS GROUP
CONVERSATION?

The Chicago Story

In a Chicago suburb, the Town Council was passing ordinances to keep Negroes from moving in. A certain pastor became concerned, especially since some members of his church were among those supporting the anti-Negro ordinances. He invited twenty-five community leaders to his home one evening, including those on both sides of the issue. Among the guests were four Negro leaders who had moved into the community before the ordinances were promoted. The host began the meeting simply by saying that a friend was going to "help us get acquainted," and that after the coffee break there was to be a discussion of the current vital subject.

In starting the session the friend who was brought in for the occasion said: "In order to get acquainted quickly, let's play a little game of matching our memories around our early experiences of work—the first work we did for which we got any pay. Where were we living then? Were we about ten or twelve years old?" The guests were all Americans from different parts of the country and from this particular suburb of Chicago. One of them a tall, good-looking, serious-faced Negro man, had grown up in South Chicago.

Several men told of paper routes they had carried. Two had dropped corn on farms and recalled the bit of folklore about the number of seeds in a hill:

> One for the blackbird, one for the crow,
> One for the cutworms, and three to grow.

They were agreeably surprised, not only that they remembered the jingle, but that it was the same in Kansas as in New Jersey. The women, both Negro and white, had had similar experiences of baby sitting or of working in the "five and tens." Several humorous experiences were related, and one sang the German lullaby taught her by her mother, that she had often used as a baby sitter. Another had been famous for her singing of "Summertime" by Gershwin.

Various kinds of experiences related to the topic of work were shared. Was Saturday night a time for fun? How did the families rest after work? And how did we spend our Sundays? All this helped the participants to relax together, to identify with one another, and to be more ready to move later into discussion of a touchy issue.

The man from South Chicago had not yet spoken.

"What about work in South Chicago when you were ten?" He spoke then, quietly and with much feeling, but not with bitterness: "I sold papers too, but I had to sell every copy before I could return at night. So I knew early in life what went on in saloons at midnight. My father had been seriously injured at work, and for ten of my growing-up years, we had only his compensation money and what mother and we children could earn." The others in the group were visibly interested as they each identified, in some way, with the image of a ten-year-old boy in such an environment. "Do you remember what you bought with the money you earned?" "Shoes," he said. "Sneakers can get pretty cold on city streets in the winter, you know."

They did not know really—not the way he did. But they were all *feeling* it now along with him.

"How did you happen to come to this community?" he was asked. "My sister at first worked here, and then she moved here. I could not, at first, understand how she could stand not being near all the people and places we were used to. And then when I came out of the army and the hospital, I stayed with her some weeks. It was then for the first time in my life that I realized what being with trees and flowers and grass and the wide open sky can do for people. I want no child of mine to grow up where I did."

They were all silent now, in that pastor's living room, as they thought of the many children still in the South Chicago of all our big cities, selling papers in the bars, running the streets at night. This group silence lasted a few minutes, as feelings of reconciliation came through, binding each participant in one of life's great mysteries. It was broken by the host's "Coffee is ready."

During the coffee break, several men pulled their chairs up close to the man from South Chicago. Were they still swapping stories of when they were ten, or talking about how they could help to make available more green spots where Negro as well as white children could grow up?

The group discussion which followed the coffee hour was to that point. The concerned fellowship was now able to get down to the real human dimensions of any housing problems—the people who work and play and live in the physical structures that shelter and nurture their love and growth as families.

The experience recounted above shows how a roomful of people, even strangers of varied backgrounds, can be helped to feel something of the warmth and trust of longtime neighbors and friends. An example of group conversation, it was aimed at getting to a dispassionate consideration of a controversial problem about which all cared passionately. We have described it briefly here to help the reader see some of the dynamics in developing a kind of compassionate give-and-take, which is central to group conversation.

Group conversation is a way of helping members of a group to experience a sense of our common humanity by first reaching back into the past for memorable experiences to be shared around a topic of universal moment or interest. The method is designed to facilitate real and spontaneous communication by developing the social climate which fosters mutual regard and confidence.

Leaders in social psychology and group procedures see group conversation as a unique and important step in the development of a group, and many have commented on the effectiveness of this simple, informal method for quickly establishing rapport. Participants are brought into greater readiness for discussion, problem solving, decision making, and other levels of social thinking and action. Because it breaks through to the feelings, group conversation leads to the kind of communication that reaches the heart of a human situation.

And we do mean heart. In our Chicago story, it is not difficult, for example, to see in the rapport and feeling tone developed, how it was possible in the discussion phase for the group to speak from the heart to the needs of all children.

Reviving a Lost Art

We have called this particular process group conversation, because that is what it is—conversation in the setting of a group. Like any other good conversation form, that much lamented lost art, it requires a willingness to share and a willingness to listen, creatively and with tenderness and firmness.

Understanding and real communication can come only in wholeness and freedom. If we reflect on these attributes, we realize that they are requisite to all human relationships, of which person-to-person conversation is a highly developed and yet spontaneous form. In the larger context of the group, however, some guidance and skill are helpful and often needed to facilitate the flow and interaction.

Not Group Discussion

Group conversation purposively structures the participation so that controversy is not invited at the outset of a meeting. The controversial aspects of an issue or problem are intentionally and actually postponed until a mood of acceptance has been developed so that the members of the group are able to enter the discussion which may follow, constructively and with a sense of trust, openness, and directness. Group discussion is deliberately polarized around issues and problems, with their pros and cons.

Most experienced leaders know that until the feeling of strangeness or suspicion, or even hostility, is cleared, little real business can be taken care of. When the feelings are complicated by differences of nationality, religion, or race, the blockages to real group development can be serious.

Interpreting New Program

Besides being merely a process to help a group feel its interrelatedness (and very often that may be the sole or primary purpose), group conversation can enable a group, such as an administrative board or staff, to move toward its larger goals. Many social work agencies, for example, sometimes find it difficult to interpret to volunteer leaders—on whom they are very largely dependent—certain aspects of their program aimed at attaining specific outcomes. Perhaps there are innovations in program which require a shift of emphasis or viewpoint in the traditional training course. A group conversation can be very helpful. An illustration may be in order.

The National Training Director of Camp Fire Girls needed to develop leaders for the Bluebird program for eight-year-olds. A Camp Fire Girls staff member describes the technique used:

> We sat down around the teatable, and I started the group conversation by asking the mothers if they remembered what they were like when they were eight years old. Mrs. G was the youngest mother and she said that all she seemed able to remember about her eighth birthday was how much she had wanted a birthday party and a big doll. But times were difficult, and her family had not been able to afford either. She remembered with great joy how her oldest sister had given her a rag doll she had made, and Mrs. G blushingly said she still had the doll. . . . Some of the

women remembered times when money had not been plentiful and clothes were made at home. One mother recalled how thrilled her family was over its first radio, and another spoke of her first ride in her uncle's new car. Mrs. T told how excited she was the first time she had made ice cream in the family's new hand freezer.

I asked the group how many of their daughters had had experiences similar to those they remembered. We all agreed that life seemed "easier" for youngsters today, but that perhaps they missed some of the fun we had had in working with our families, in learning how to do many things. Mrs. S recalled the fun her family had while singing as they all worked together in her father's small store. A penny had seemed important then; today, money did not have the same meaning to her daughter. The rest agreed, and they all felt that we should help our girls to learn something about the value of money as well as how to get along with each other. One of the mothers said that with school work, dancing lessons, music lessons, favorite radio and TV programs, and playing out of doors, the girls rarely had time for doing things at home. I was happy that I could tell them that as Bluebirds the girls would be learning to work together and would be learning something of the value of money. They had already decided to contribute pennies to make a group gift to the UNICEF Milk Fund.

After our group conversation, the women were enthusiastic about the program, and each volunteered whatever talent she had—some to drive cars for outings, others to teach the girls skills such as cooking, swimming, and crafts. . . . It seemed to me as if we had suddenly discovered talent in abundance! [1]

These two illustrations of the Chicago suburb and the Bluebird leaders serve to explain what group conversation is and how it helps to remove certain barriers to good group communication and relationships. We shall see now what some of these barriers are and how group conversation may help to overcome them.

NOTES FOR CHAPTER 1

1. Adapted with permission of Camp Fire Girls, Inc., from "Have You Tried Remembering Together?" by Marva Andrews Stuart, *The Camp Fire Girl,* March, 1955.

2 : BARRIERS TO GOOD COMMUNICATION

All of us who have any responsibility for group leadership—whether it be in general or adult education, in religious education, in youth work, or in industry—come up at some time or another against a wall of misunderstanding. So often people do not really listen to one another. They hear only the words and not the person behind the words. The problem is one of communication in depth. The pressures of life have made us build protective coverings around our true selves. It is difficult for us to communicate through this shell, on whichever side of it we happen to be.

If there are those present who have any kind of authority over us—the principal of the school, the boss of the factory, the director of the conference—we feel we must not let down our guard, we must say only what we are expected to say. If there are strangers in the group, we become cautious and wonder if we can trust them. Of course, the others have similar feelings—the boss, the principal, the director, the stranger—each feels the same inhibition. Each, too, must act as he is expected to act, or perhaps not act at all.

Yet, it is to the interest of each person, and to the work or the cause to which the members of the group are committed, that as quickly as possible, they share their experiences, their feelings, and their thinking. The experiences and the thinking of each member are unique and are needed in the final group outcome.

The barriers to communication are often due to differences in status, in age, in racial, religious, cultural, and even regional backgrounds. Group conversation can help to break through these barriers if we are careful to plan thoughtfully our approach to them. We need to be helped as a group to ask: What is it that blocks us? What closes our eyes to the reality of the other person? What is it that closes our ears to his feelings?

The exchange must bring a genuine sense of relatedness if it is to help a group get to work at a level which would take them directly to the real issues at hand. Differences in background or status must be recognized and accepted to bring into the group a feeling of unity, of being a team. Let us look at some of the barriers.

BARRIERS of Cultural Backgrounds

Americans are a people of peoples. Cultural pluralism has been characteristic of our population picture from the beginning. Each new war or crisis has brought its wave of immigrants or refugees. Even today we are not without our newcomers who seek a welcome for their patterns. The members of each new group have had to become "good Americans" by conforming. What to conform to, however, could not be fully defined.

Was it enough to cut oneself off from the political past? It seemed also imperative to deny one's cultural background and heritage. In that denial millions of Americans have become alienated from a part of themselves. With the alienation has come a sense of insecurity and fragmentation.

In rejecting the cultural past, one has turned one's back on psychic sources in which is rooted the inner reality that renews. Unless one can make use of these emotional resources, one is handicapped as one reaches out for satisfying experiences and mature relations with other people.

New waves of immigrants, however, often so overwhelm the communities into which they come, that old-time residents react only with negative feelings of fear, suspicion, hostility. If the newcomer is given opportunity to share his cultural best, his patterns not only may heighten the color and drama of our neighborhoods, but can carry universal components of emotion and spirituality which are healing and sustaining for us all. Barriers of distrust and prejudice can be overcome, and we learn to enjoy the uniqueness of our new neighbors. This happened in

a New York City school at the height of the Puerto
Rican migration into the metropolis.

Outbreaks of teen-age gang violence and adult
prejudice all but destroyed the Parents Association
until it was helped to develop a school-home project,
which ran for four years. The whole neighborhood
was caught up in the spirit and activities that were
built around group conversation as a central approach. A number of mothers were trained to lead
the conversations. The Puerto Rican pattern of the
parranda or progressive party was adopted as the
occasion for each intercultural exchange. The group
conversation format was accommodated to the goals
and situation of the project for which the Parents
Association had the support of the school and the
Board of Education. Every child in the seventh grade
and, directly or indirectly, his family and his teachers were involved in the undertaking.[1]

The reader should understand that each weekly
parranda was supplemented by other activities in
social studies, in English and art classes. The project
was reflected in assembly programs, extracurricular
activities, and finally in an all-community festival at
the end of each school year.

As the mothers in the school worked together,
they came to see, in the mobility of the American
people, the need for all families to carry with them,
as they move into new areas, something at least symbolic of their past. As the noted social psychologist,
Lawrence K. Frank, put it in appraising the project,

"We have then to consider the need to do for our day what our ancestors did for theirs: to create a new way of doing things together in family groups which give meaning to life."

What are the equivalents today of such sustaining experiences as the trip to grandmother's at Thanksgiving, the family lighting of candles, and gift giving in the different religious festivals, or of the ways our ancestors celebrated the coming of spring? This group of mothers, sensitized to the spiritual sustenance they enjoy from such experiences in their own backgrounds, asked how they might build family strength with new rituals to meet today's needs. Will there be a way to develop and uphold enduring values as we move into the new world of our children?

. . . of Age

Teen years are hard years. One of the most heartbreaking problems of today is the lack of communication between teen-agers and their elders. Teen-agers are often as embarrassed to discuss even with their peers matters of deep concern.

If we can find new group structures that will enable us to communicate what we really feel—our failures, our fears and anxieties, as well as our joys and aspirations—it will be easier to produce the social cement that can hold our society together. It has been possible to release teen-agers to share such feelings if the group is small and led by an adult who inspires confidence and trust.

Those who work with youth groups sometimes find it difficult to get below the surface in relationships. "Communication" is often a fruitful topic of conversation with groups of teen-agers. In one case, the leader started off with her memory of the special doll she loved as a child, and still keeps. After a few such recollections, the group was asked to share memories of a pet they had had, to which they had felt close. How did the pet express its responses? Can we share memories of the first close pal of our own age and something of our feelings? Then, too, who was the grownup to whom we felt closest—a parent, grandparent, teacher, neighbor? As we look back, which experience was a two-way process, in which we were also giving of ourselves?

This led to a valuable sharing around the importance of the individual: that each is unique, yet each is a part of that which is divine and which binds humanity together. The group experience was kept on the spontaneous sharing of pertinent experiences, questions, doubts, with no attempt to find answers. It helped the participants to look at how they communicate with others within the family or outside of it, through spontaneous play, artistic endeavors, or work. Girl-boy relationships were seen as an area of communication which could enrich and fulfill one's life. The group looked at the religious process as communication with one's higher self and with God. Here are two comments from teen-age participants:

> "I've never had a religious feeling. Because I was forced by my parents to go to church, I got nothing out of it."

> "At a work camp last summer, I'm quite sure I had what can be called a religious feeling—it was a feeling of togetherness—we were painting the side of a shed, and I could feel inside the people I was working with, and even inside the tools I used."

At one teen-age camp conference, the topic for the group conversation was "Red Letter Days." After a few minutes of sharing positive experiences this question was asked: "What was the first time, or the time you remember most vividly, when you were punished at home or at school? How did you feel about it?" One boy had said that he could get away with anything, fool his parents, and talk his way out of anything, and therefore he felt safe. Another observed: "When you fool your parents you feel safe, but you aren't as safe as you would be if you had been caught and learned something. We need the protection of older people until we have had enough experience of our own to know what is dangerous and what isn't."

This kind of sharing takes place more easily among people of the same age, but it is especially valuable when it can happen in a group of mixed ages.

In a Temple Sisterhood, age differences were compounded by the fact that most of the older women had been brought up in "the old country." The Rabbi's wife led a group conversation around memories of "Bread," and what families did to give a sense of security. The sharing of food memories, symbolism, song, humor, hospitality patterns, as well as the deeper aspect of family festivals, was not only fascinating to the younger women, but meaningful. As the women compared these recollections from the old countries with activities in their families today, they were able to respond more openly to each other, and to their Rabbi's challenging question, "How shall we perform rites today that will give us the morale, the courage, the faith, the hope, the patterns to keep on working for a better world, though we see the world not yet responding?"

Anxiety is common to us all. In one group conversation some twenty Quakers were sharing their most persistent worries. The sixty-fivers, outwardly comfortable and seeming to have no anxieties, confessed that they dreaded being dependent on others. They feared not being able to make new and satisfying friendships to take the place of "those who have gone on." The young married couples were worried about having sufficient income to maintain "our standard of living and send our children through college." The oldsters then turned to listen to the anxieties of three teen-agers in the group: "I wonder if I'll get on the right path in life." "Will I find the right life partner?" What was learned in that mixed-age group is that anxiety is common to us all and each age level has its own particular kind. The feeling of unity in the silence which followed the sharing was proof, too, that although anxieties can be divisive, shared anxieties in an atmosphere of love can unite a group.

Wisdom needs to be shared. Mixed-age groups are valuable for the sharing of wisdom—the kind of wisdom that comes only from having lived it. But who should listen to this wisdom if not the less aged? And where should it be found if not in family life? Our culture today has lost the structures for this sharing. In a few families it still goes on. Many Irish-Americans, even to the fourth generation, have times when the old folk tell the old, old stories.

An American Indian, now a music teacher in the schools of a midwestern city, said that because in his tribe all old people were grandparents to every child, his father—after the family moved to a city—would invite, once a year, an old person from the Reservation to spend a week with the family to tell the old tales of wisdom.

. . . of Race

Sometimes, in periods of social stress, when many people express the increase in fears and prejudices around them, the organizations to which they belong also reflect the strain. Because of intergroup fears and prejudices, the wires of communication among

members of a group or an organization are o en
completely cut or they become meaningless. he
group in which such communication is interrupte is
without a solid and continuing core of members v o
feel personally identified and committed to its p o-
gram. In this situation, a well-led group conversati 1
may help members begin to relate to this comm
ment. It may re-establish communication lines
that the members are motivated to work effective
again in the organization of which they are a pai

As an illustration—the white and Negro mothe
in a northern suburban PTA seemed to be workin
smoothly in their school. However, some of th
Negro mothers sensed that all was not well belov
the surface. Their own children came home reporting classroom incidents which they interpreted as
bias on the part of some teachers. The white mothers
on the Executive Committee of the PTA first realized
this problem when it was shared in a group conversation. The forty mothers, plus the principal and a few
teachers who recalled "our own schooldays," were a
good cross section of the religious and cultural
groups represented in the school. Their shared memories enabled them to face with real honesty the
question, "What about our children today? How do
they feel in this school?" When all the parents and
teachers recognized that they were involved, they
could look more realistically at the intergroup attitudes and problems reflected in their school, their
homes, and their community.

Breakthrough in the South. That communication on certain levels between white and Negro citizens in the South has lessened since the Supreme Court decision, is well known. What is not so well known is the amount of communication of a more understanding kind between deeply concerned people that does not necessarily get into the news.

Group conversation has been used in Florida,[2] Georgia, and Virginia. Best results come from an indirect approach: that is, a mixed group brought together for a reason other than race. In Atlanta, it was to welcome some exchange students from Africa. After matching or contrasting their memories of clocks, and their concept of time as expressed in family activities, the group found similar memories, in Africa and in our South, of both white and Negro grandparents telling the same folk tales. Folk tales seem a far cry from the need to do something to prevent an integration crisis from erupting. But is it not true that people who have met each other in a face-to-face situation of confidence and trust are the individuals who are more likely to join hands when the crisis comes? If enough have joined hands, then perhaps the crisis can be avoided.

. . . of Social Walls

In an article in the *New York Times* the question was asked:

Why do so few Negro families buy homes in suburbs where by now public opinion, in these northern communities, is on their side? The climate has been altered in the last decade by the many fair-housing groups, the distribution of open-occupancy pledges, wholesale mailing of literature, public meetings, private persuasion, and the listing of homes available to Negroes.[3]

In a Long Island community, all the steps above had been taken, and a Negro family moved into an all-white neighborhood. But the most necessary step —that of merely being neighborly—was not taken, or the following could not have been said: "We've lived as the only Negro family on this suburban street for two years now, and no one ever speaks to us when we go out in the morning or come home at night."

Social isolation and anonymity are concomitants today of most city and suburban life and are not limited to attitudes toward Negroes or other minority peoples. In the huge City Housing projects large aggregations of people are storied on top of each other, with little intervisiting in homes. In the split-level developments mushrooming in our suburbs there is for the most part the same lack of neighborliness. To be sure, their Christian churches and Jewish temples are busy finding their "own people" in these towns; but, in the finding, new barriers of isolation are often created.

It was partly to answer this need for interhome visiting that the Bronx River Community Center of the Jewish Association for Neighborhood Centers, in co-operation with the New York City Housing Authority and the Bronx Young Women's Christian Association, developed an intercultural program serving all groups in the neighborhood. A low-income public housing project had come into a heretofore highly stable, middle-income Jewish neighborhood, bringing in other population groups including Negroes and Puerto Ricans. It was the first time the residents had had to adjust to significant economic, social, and ethnic differences. Social and psychological distance between the old and the new communities grew to the point of isolation, with attitudes of apathy, fear, and hostility. Leaders, alert to impending difficulties, came together in an effort to avert irreparable harm to the newly extended neighborhood. Professional and volunteer workers were trained to lead group conversations and encouraged to hold social gatherings in one another's homes and invite their new neighbors in.

. . . of Language

In a New York City Parents Association, the problem of relationship was hampered by language differences. Because of the large number of non-English-speaking Puerto Rican parents, the principal of the school and the Parents Association leaders found it impossible to give the parents information about school affairs, except the barest necessary facts translated into Spanish. Certainly no feeling of relatedness could develop from a cursory doling out of admonitions.

The project started with training a few of the mothers to use group conversation. Mothers who brought their kindergarten and first-grade children to school at 9 o'clock in the morning, were invited to meet weekly at coffee. A running group conversation on subjects of immediate interest to the group was conducted. Whispered translations in Spanish or English went on simultaneously at each table. Perhaps the topic was the different ways fall festivals were celebrated by nationalities represented in the group. The newcomers—did they need to have the "Trick or Treat" project of the United Nations explained to them? The conversation might be interrupted by the president of the Parents Association or the principal of the school who wished to make some announcements, or to explain facts or situations or services that the parents ought to know about. In this way the newcomers learned for instance, of the city's health and other social services.

While they were at the coffee tables, the women worked together with their hands, making useful things to be given to those in need. When a baby was born to a mother in the group, a Baby Festival was held to which the mother brought her three-weeks-old baby. The mothers sang one another's lullabies in different languages, comparing customs of naming children and presenting their gifts for the baby. Cross-cultural friendships were made.

Learning English can be fun. Newcomers to America tend to pass through too long a period of isolation from older Americans. It is natural, of course, that when large numbers come together as "waves of immigrants," they want to be near those whom they can understand and feel close to. Church and community leaders who have sponsored immigrant families sometimes do not know how to reach below the outward cultural differences to the bedrock of mutual concerns. When this basic kinship has been discovered, the sharing of differences can become an exciting adventure for both old and new Americans. One experience in a group conversation made a world of difference to a newcomer, who wrote in her English class:

> "I told my family: 'Just think, me sitting in the circle of such very educated people, and no one acted like they were better than the other person.' It made me feel so relaxed, I felt like I knew all the other members for a long time."

The effect of such experiences on those who *teach* English should be stressed, too:

> "It has given me a great appreciation of what they [the newcomers] have to give to American life. It is so easy for us to feel superior, teaching English to those who don't know it; but when we share our memories like this, it gives us the opportunity to see that our foreign born are superior to us in some things, and hence our fellowship can be on a give-and-take basis."

Language need not be a barrier. If and when a group conversation leader is not sufficiently adept in a language to conduct a conversation which is based on spontaneity, it has been possible to use two interpreters instead of one. This was first done in Germany, later in Mexico; it took place in New York City, with a mixed group including a large proportion of non-English-speaking refugee Chinese.

The success, however, depends on most of the group knowing the language of the leader when it is spoken slowly and distinctly, though possibly not being able to speak it themselves. Always, of course, there will be a few who understand nothing of the leader's language. This latter group of perhaps six or seven can be reached by being seated in a huddle in the far part of the circle, with an interpreter in their midst who carries on a continuous whispered translation, while the leader clearly speaks his own tongue. All are asked to respond to the pump-priming questions in their own language, and the leader has a second interpreter close to his ear. The group conversation can then proceed smoothly and spontaneously, with no loss of feeling tone by waiting for translations.

. . . of Desks

To understand others, one must understand himself. The need may be for a faculty to look at one of the deeper challenges in education today, such as helping pupils to understand themselves. Unless the individual teacher is reached emotionally, an intellectual, high-minded didaction of principles is not enough to motivate change in his approach to their work.

A group conversation, such as one in a school near the nation's capital, helped some sixty teachers to share experiences from their own educational memories. There was a striking change in mood as each person came out of hiding to tell of a teacher who had blocked him, or of one who had released him. This conversation made emotionally salient the needs of students to know themselves. More important, it helped those present to understand Jersild's contention that the teacher who wants to help his pupils understand themselves must constantly strive to understand himself.[4] A participant wrote of the session:

> "It was fun and relaxing, and yet we saw each other, as well as our pupils, in a different light. Certainly our roles as teachers came clearer to each of us at the end of the hour, when we asked ourselves those pertinent questions about education today."

. . . of Strangeness

If it is the first staff meeting of the year, with several new members, the barrier may be mainly one of strangeness. There is little time today for the kind of social activity in which fellowship can develop. With this need in mind a Young Women's Christian Association's city-wide staff of fifty started its September meeting with autumn memories. Here is the executive director's evaluation:

> "Too often a staff is so bogged down with the mechanics of program and details of necessary business, that the element of fellowship is neglected. We feel that the spirit of unity that was brought out by means of group conversation at our first meeting of the year will stay with us through the coming months."

... of Faith

Americans tend to forget that there are other kinds of religions in our midst than Christianity and Judaism. However, the lack of communication between these two major religions in our country is serious. After more than a quarter of a century of emphasis put by national organizations on the need for providing interfaith experiences, the number of Christian churches that take the initiative in inviting members of nearby synagogues to a social gathering is all too few. An annual interfaith luncheon is not enough to develop the kind of communication between Jew and Christian that will make unnecessary such special efforts at developing mutual understanding. The training for this kind of communication on the part of pastors and rabbis is indicated:

> The Colgate-Rochester Divinity School wanted to introduce its student pastors to effective ways of developing interfaith activities in the local community. Training of a group of pastors was followed by help-

ing them to start programs of group conversations in the churches they were serving. Rewarding experience around the seasonal festivals with their neighbors from nearby synagogues helped participants to see the need for extending interfaith activities beyond a single contact or a yearly event.

There may be other faiths represented among participants in some of the group conversations, but they, too, whether they be Buddhist or Mohammedan, Confucian or Indian-American, will have similar customs at each season with interesting differences. In this connection we bear in mind that we are not trying to start a new or combined one-world religion. Our differences are valuable and need to be understood and respected. Sharing our various patterns of saying grace or celebrating a season does not mean adopting the other person's religion. It is an experience in intercultural understanding sorely needed in our culturally diverse country. It is the development of mutual respect and appreciation that is important.

The national secretaries of the Christian Friendliness Department and the Women's Division of the American Baptist Convention had difficulty in interpreting their new program toward the goal of a more inclusive fellowship in local church groups. They were concerned about the increasing number of foreign students and refugees in their communities, many of whom were socially isolated. There was also the need for sending city children to rural homes for vacation, and the need to bring Negro and white Baptists into one fellowship. Group conversations were held in strategic spots around the country as an introduction. Pilot training workshops were set up by National Board members to develop a cadre of leaders who could demonstrate and train others in the use of the method. Teams went into each of the area-training conferences across their thirty-four state conventions to reach leaders functioning in local churches. They, too, were given training so that they could take the method into their parish groups.[6]

The statistics from the 1959-1961 Annual Reports of the National Council of American Baptist Women show that this widespread use of group conversation is now affecting other phases of their work. Their 1961 Annual Report shows that group conversation was used 3,303 times in 929 churches. There were 6,846 invited guests and 20,838 church members involved.

. . . of Lack of Time

Then again, the difficulty in a particular church or club, of relating closely to one another, may be mainly the result of pressures of modern life which give less and less time for the normal social interaction of people that is so basic to communication.

The Religious Society of Friends has adapted the group conversation method to what is termed the "Quaker Dialogue." [5] Over a hundred groups in various parts of the country have participated in the use of this method. It is directed toward helping these local groups of Friends share informally their ideas and deep concerns on certain aspects of their religious life. The same group of not more than twenty-two attend all three of the two-hour sessions. Recent comments of participants show not only an increase of deeper communication within the group, but more participation in their Friends' Meeting activities.

... of Staff Status

In some organizations or businesses, management and employees seldom meet on any but strictly business committees, which include only a small portion of the group. When an event like the staff celebration of a holiday or the approaching wedding of one of its members takes place, little is done to help individuals to relate to one another in any meaningful way.

Instead of the customary "booze party" in a dress factory the afternoon before Christmas, the chairman of the Education Committee of the International Ladies Garment Workers Union planned a celebration of "Our Winter Festivals" through a group conversation.

"After that party in our shop," commented the Education Committee chairman, "not only did we all become better friends, but several joined our Education Committee. It was easier for me, too, to settle wage schedules later with the boss, for he was at the party."

. . . *of Illness*

Being sick is being different, too. The patients in Ward A of a hospital for chronic diseases had been there a long time. By now they indulged in much quarreling and griping about the hospital's care and food.

On Thanksgiving Day, there was to be a group conversation for as many patients as could comfortably assemble in the solarium of that floor. They came in wheel chairs, in beds, and on crutches; a few walked.

"I can't remember anything. It was too long ago when I was a child in Italy," was the negative response of the stout woman in a wheel chair. "Were you ever serenaded when you were a girl?" "Of course," came the answer with a smile of remembrance.

"And did you ever do any serenading?" the leader asked a man in pajamas who said he had grown up in Genoa. "Of course," was his quick reply. "Then let's both go and serenade her now." Immediately he was in front of the wheel chair, and so was the leader. With her hands the leader bowed the violin in pantomime, until the man, in memory, took up in imagination his own musical instrument. Then the leader beckoned all to join in singing "Maria."

But that was only one episode of the spontaneous, unconscious role playing of early years which continued for over an hour, with six nurses and two doctors also participating. They could see that re-membering together pleasant experiences of youth released the forces of both physical and psychical healing. One of the patients summed up well the experience: "I want to say that I am thankful for the way we are cared for in this hospital, but this after-noon has done me more good than the doctor's medi-cine."

. . . of Nationality

Now that the State Department of our government and other agencies are preparing many Americans for their roles abroad by trying to help them to un-derstand and cope with the *differences* in culture, it might be wise also to introduce them to a technique for finding basic *similarities* in "their" and "our" ways of doing things. Besides, how much richer and more satisfying it is for all when these international arrangements, including our Peace Corps, are two-way sharing experiences.

Relating our socially valuable cultural differences is a subject which needs more exploration in groups with people from different countries. Our concern about international and political and economic mat-ters is immediate and necessary. Basic to it should be a deep concern to help those who travel, to experi-ence and evaluate culture patterns of another coun-try including values that concern child rearing, time sense, and work attitudes. There may be, among these, ways we might want to adopt or adapt in our own home situation. They may give us a basis for looking more critically at and holding onto that which truly makes us what we are.

In one group conversation, a student from Egypt said: "This one hour has given me more of a picture of American life than my whole year here of chance experiences." Hostesses often feel uncomfortable about entertaining foreign students in their homes. "I understand that most of them are graduate students, doctors, or government officials. What can we talk about?" After such a social time one hostess remarked: "Now I look forward to having two foreign students in my home tomorrow."

Most foreign students are interested in our folklore, and they know their own, but rarely find an opportunity of sharing theirs or learning ours. Group conversation provides this opportunity, and when the participants sense the similarities in folk songs and folklore, the shared feeling of unity is deeper and more lasting.

When the barrier is clearly one of nationality differences, as in the many kinds of international services and centers now opening up in many parts of the world, communication—because of language and other differences—may be even more difficult to establish. When people of different backgrounds combine learning each other's language with a sincere but conscious attempt to share and understand at least some of the social values back of their customs, deeper communication can be facilitated.

After World War II, for example, there was opportunity and need in West Germany to help leaders change the authoritative pattern intensified during the Hitler period. They needed help to realize that in their parent and other community groups, members could make decisions of their own, and that they need not always wait for someone higher up to tell them what to do.

In a U.S. State Department sponsored program, German leaders were trained in the use of group conversation to take the memories of their people back beyond war experiences to their childhood impressions of love, acceptance, and security. With careful preparation the leaders were able to help others to accept and to integrate psychologically their more recent experiences. Thus, in a group conversation on "Special Days of My Youth," came memories, first of fascinating birthday parties when so much love and feeling of importance were showered upon the child. After a few such memories came this one: "But the most wonderful birthday for me was in camp, when no cake was to be had for love or money. Finally, someone found a single cracker, and around this we sang our songs and gave our love and blessings."

After sharing their memories of the Advent and Christmas season, one woman (she was one of twelve million expellees who had been thrust on West Germany by the Potsdam Agreement) offered this: "I landed, a complete stranger, on a Marburg street with two suitcases and three small children. It was Christmas Eve, and no home, no tree. Finally, an attic was secured for us, and that one little pine bough which we put up in the corner is what I shall never forget."

We see, in the examples given above, how group conversation helped to break through different kinds of barriers to communication, and to bring the participants into a mood in which they could more easily relate to each other as well as to their inner selves. Whether it is a group of mixed backgrounds or of a more homogeneous make-up, it is these barriers of relationships that must be overcome before there can be a release of the participants to work together as a group on whatever problem is at hand. These may be relationships between persons or they may be relationships that they have to make within themselves. On whichever level they come, problems in relationship may operate to the disadvantage of the entire group or to particular members if a way is not opened to their proper solution. Group conversation aims to release participants to deal with these problems.

NOTES FOR CHAPTER 2

1. The staff of the Workshop for Cultural Democracy trained the parent leaders and acted as consultants throughout the program. For full report see Rachel Davis Dubois, *Neighbors in Action* (New York: Harper & Brothers, 1950).

2. In Miami, Daytona Beach, and Palm Beach, there have been biracial Training Workshops in Group Conversation which included volunteers from United Church Women, Temple Sisterhood, Society of Friends, and the Florida section of the National Conference of Christians and Jews.

3. *New York Times,* Dec. 5, 1961.

4. "All the teacher's relationships with his pupils, the feeling he has toward them, the judgments he passes on them, the ways in which he rewards and punishes, praises and blames, acknowledges and ignores are charged with psychic meaning." This statement was made by Arthur Jersild, in *In Search of Life* (New York: Bureau of Publications, Teachers College, Columbia University, 1952).

5. For more information write the Friends General Conference, 1515 Cherry St., Philadelphia, Pa., which publishes a *Handbook for Leaders of Quaker Dialogues.*

6. A manual was prepared with the staff of the Workshop for Cultural Democracy. *Around the World with Group Conversation* can be secured from the American Baptist Home Mission Society, Valley Forge, Pa.

3 : HOW TO LEAD A GROUP CONVERSATION

The leading of group conversation is an art, and as such it inheres in a climate of spontaneity and freedom. Too, as in all other art forms, there are definite techniques and disciplines. These will be explained in this chapter so that the leader may become familiar with them before developing his own style or attempting improvisations.

No artist succeeds who does not love his materials. Just so, the group conversation leader must love people, all kinds of people. We expect of him a sensitivity to persons and their personality needs, and artistry in handling his subject. In group conversation nothing is so important as helping all participants to feel comfortable and accepted so that each can take part spontaneously and contribute to the creativity and growth of the group. Here then the aim is to help each person communicate more easily and to build a group spirit which allows each one to be himself.

In other words, the leader should be warm and outgoing. He should be able to absorb hostility, if it happens to come up, without becoming defensive. He should not be one who will be tempted to use the openness of the situation for his own or another's intellectualizing or pontificating. Nor should he be one who will seek to take over or dominate a group. Rather, he must be able to feel joy in "the satisfaction of stimulating others to learn and to share the process of becoming a more adequate group member himself . . . to feel secure in oneself and in the group itself, to be able to try out new ways and not to be upset if puzzling situations develop; to notice what is happening to the group, to be flexible in one's role and at the same time to appraise one's self thoughtfully or to accept constructive, sincere criticism from another." [1]

Though it is not always possible, it would be well if one could first experience a group conversation before trying to lead one. The next best thing would be to study the description of one that has taken place. We narrate here another group conversation, before we take up the technical steps, one by one. Chapter 4 will offer further examples and discussion of the steps involved. The experience described below took place in a culturally mixed group, and it will be seen that its basic structure is easily identifiable.

"I Don't Belong Here"

The sixth-grade pupils had invited their mothers to a class party. Along with the other women, the group conversation leader had come to the school. One, when she saw two Negro women and four or five Puerto Rican mothers, started to frown and leave, saying, "I don't belong here." "Why not?" whispered the leader, not yet introduced. "I wasn't brought up with such people." "Where were you brought up?" "In Iowa." "Oh, I'm old-line American, too, but I think we'll have a good time; let's go in together."

About twenty-five pupils came into the front seats, as the fifteen mothers formed a circle. The school principal introduced the leader as the one who would start the group in a game. The conversation went more or less as follows:

"All games have an element of make-believe, so let's make believe we are all the same age." On this occasion, in order to insure more adult than child participation, the leader asked the children to play the role of ghosts listening in to what their parents were doing when they were the same age. "How old are you?" the leader asked, pointing to several pupils. "Eleven," was the answer. Quickly turning to the parents, the leader said: "We are eleven years old now. Where are we? As for myself, I am on a farm in South Jersey." Others were in five different states, besides New York, one in Canada, four in

Puerto Rico, one in Germany, one in Russia, one in Italy, and two in New York City. "What do we like to do, or how do we feel about this time of year? On my farm, we are sick and tired of winter as it gets near February, and I am looking forward to groundhog day."

Mrs. Iowa had a wonderful time, as she described the winds of Iowa, and we shivered with sympathy for the woman from Canada. Soon the Puerto Ricans were saying, "We don't have winter." "No, but what do you do at this time of year?" Out came memories of *Carnivale*, and soon the whole group, parents and children, assisted by the pianist, was humming with the Puerto Ricans one of their songs.

"Who else has special celebrations in early spring?" The Italian-American mother then told of the St. Joseph parties in her family. Mouths watered as she described the delicious foods prepared for them. With only a little coaxing, she danced a bit of the *tarantella*. All the group took part in some way, by singing or hand clapping if not by dancing.

"Does any other group at this time of year have special songs, dances, foods?" The two Jewish mothers from Germany and Russia told of their jolly *Purim* memories and reminded the others that the *Purim* Festival is based on the dramatic story in the Book of Esther. By this time, the entire group could see that what is common to all cultures in the early spring is the universal spirit of release. They also could see the interesting differences among the ways in which this spirit is expressed.

At the end of the hour, Mrs. Iowa was asked with what song it would be good to close. She replied with deep feeling, "I think we ought to sing 'God Bless America.'" The feeling of mutual acceptance in the group was now evident. The song was sung, and *hamantaschen* and other cakes which the mothers had brought were served.

Mrs. Iowa's change in attitude, of course, now needed to be reinforced by other positive experiences. However, the fact that she later joined the PTA and began to function on its committees gives us great faith in the sociological principle that attitudes are mainly formed by social contacts, and that social contacts can do much to change them. Certainly, too, Mrs. Iowa was not a bigot; we now know that for bigots only deep psychiatry or a "miracle of God" would be adequate. She does represent the millions of people in our land who, according to Professor Stone of Vassar, have "the kind of prejudice which has been learned in simple, casual ways reflecting the social atmosphere in which they have grown up." [2]

Spring Belongs to Everyone

Although there are many kinds of topics for group conversations, such as Work, Red-Letter Days, First Journey Away from Home—in fact, any universal experience—we shall use the seasonal theme to show

how a group conversation is led. The structure, content, and aesthetic elements involved are more easily made clear.

Seasonal topics are easy for the novice. Because cultures all over the world celebrate the changing seasons, participants generally respond readily. We need to remember that even if they are removed by two or three generations from early folk festivals, some remnants have been handed down in many families. However, we must be mindful that the increasing pressures toward conformity in American life are robbing many homes of this rich heritage.

Invariably in group conversation people are pleased when they can connect some custom, be it a recipe, a bit of folklore, song, or dance, to a time when it was meaningful in their own life or in the lives of their families. An example is the "Here We Go, Looby Loo" dance of our children. Most of us have forgotten that it was a frontier dance celebrating the Saturday night bath. Another example is the "Go Tell Aunt Rhody" jingle about the old gray goose, which reminds us of feather beds.

It is a gift, then, when there are present a few grandparents either who were immigrants or who grew up in homes which keep some of the Old World customs. For instance, most American Jews as children experienced—and many families still carry on, though not all—their colorful seasonal family festivals. It can be enriching for non-Jews to hear of these experiences in the context of a well-conducted group conversation.

If the goal is related to the development of understanding and accepting each other among people of various regional, cultural, or national backgrounds, a seasonal topic will be natural. Autumn as a theme can be used from the first of September up to Thanksgiving but, after that date, everybody is ready for winter memories. Around February 1, we long to talk about early spring. Just before Easter, we are ready for late spring memories, and along about the middle of May we are thinking of summer.

The question arises as to whether, in the one-season regions of our country, people would respond to seasonal topics. Our experience has been that there are many migrants who have a nostalgic memory of the seasons. We must remember that the tropics have different kinds of seasons—wet and dry, for instance. Students and others from tropical countries have been very interesting participants in group conversations when they related how they felt and what they did during changes in these seasons in their country.

As seen by our example of group conversation, the leader holds in mind a few "pump-priming" or lead questions which he uses to structure the sharing. How he uses these with the co-operation of his co-leaders, we shall show later. Here we offer a basic pattern for categories of lead questions which have been used with consistent success. They build on one another and can lead dramatically to a significant close:

- Memories that involve the senses—the feel, smells, tastes, sounds, colors.
- Memories of fun we had with other children in home and at school at that time of the year, such as games, trips, and special events.
- Memories of what we did in our homes or schools, or in churches or synagogues.

The sharing of experiences and feelings from these categories should then be channeled into a meaningful ending.

The psychological reasons for these questions are easily seen. Memories connected with the senses are close to the threshold of consciousness, so these are drawn first. From the sensory experiences, the next most natural area for easy sharing we have found to be that of memories of fun with other children. Most participants recall with vivid excitement these early play events in their neighborhoods or school. The experiences we had with our families have deep meanings for us, and sharing such cherished memories builds toward a significant group feeling. These events may have taken place in home, church or synagogue, or community. The rapport which grows out of the sharing of such tender material can lead the group to a high feeling level, and can be channeled into a mood of commitment which builds toward a meaningful ending. The how and when of the ending we shall discuss later.

Off on a Group Conversation

At this point the leader will want to know how to introduce the idea of group conversation to new participants. This of course depends on the nature of the group and the reason for its coming together. If it is for a social time, then the idea can be introduced simply as a game of matching memories, though, of course, it is more than a game. For intragroup and intrapersonal situations, a different reason is given, as, in a religiously motivated group, it might be: "Since in a few moments we want to talk about our religious concerns, shall we start by sharing certain of our earliest religious memories in the broadest sense of the term."

A more sophisticated group of professional people may want to have some prestige attached to the sharing which at first may seem a naïve thing to need. One might quote Harry Overstreet, who, after participating in a group conversation, remarked: "Mature adults should come together more often for the sake of enjoying one another, and for the relaxation of doing things that have the life-sustaining seriousness of play." Our experience in leading hundreds of these group conversations is that with few exceptions persons are easily caught up in the mood of spontaneous give-and-take.

Assuming that a group of twenty to forty people

are in the circle of one's living room or church or club parlor, and that a few co-leaders have co-operated in thinking through something of what might take place, how does one start?

The leader may begin by assuring the group, if they are mainly strangers, that the purpose of the gathering is to become better acquainted and to relax and have a good time together. He may say something to this effect: "This is not a group discussion, such as we have when there is a problem to be considered, but group conversation, which is simply a way of matching our common experiences around a universal topic. A kind of game, if you wish, with a couple of rules. When one person is giving his or her memories, the rest of us will find our own memories also bubbling over. I'll know by the expression on your face or the wave of your hand that you want to come next. Then, too, since singing together is relaxing, if anyone thinks of a song that matches a memory, mention it. If we know it, we'll sing it; if not, we'll skip it. Or we may even try a bit of folk dance if the urge comes to us. And lastly, since we want everyone to have the opportunity to talk, no one of us can talk too long. Shall we start matching our memories of what we liked to do long ago, at this season of the year?"

Help your participants recall where they were at eight or ten or twelve years of age. This is psychologically invaluable. It helps even the most shy to try his voice out before the group in a way that brings him a feeling of recognition and acceptance. It also helps the leader, who should make a special effort to remember what regions and countries are represented. He can later draw in certain memories from, let us say, France or California to round out the memory picture, or casually to invite the participation of the timid. This placing should come *after* the group has been given an explanation of what is to be done. They can then see the reason for it. The leader might proceed by saying, "First, we had better say who we are and where we were at the age of ten, twelve, or fourteen, since that is the age which will most easily bring out our similar memories."

"I was growing up in New York City. Where were you? Let's go quickly around the circle telling where we were at that age. This will be the only time we shall go clockwise; after this, our sharing will be completely spontaneous." This last statement gives assurance to the reticent. In the placing, if someone eagerly starts on memories, the leader can tactfully interrupt and say that our memories will come later, and repeat his original statement that we are telling where we were at the age of ten or twelve or thereabouts. The leader may lighten the recital of place with a few remarks. Humor is to be encouraged.

During the placing, too, the leader may say: "I hope we have someone here who was born abroad, for that will make our meeting even more interesting." If a few children are present, one may be given the role of counting the states and countries from which people have come.

The leader sits where he can see the faces of all the participants. If the group happens to be large—that is, thirty or more—the leader may find it natural to leave his chair occasionally, and move about in the center as he encourages people to take part. There is no need to be unduly concerned about a momentary feeling of unnaturalness at the start. This is usual with any meeting of strangers.

The placing done, the leader starts, in order to set the pattern so that others will know what is expected, with his own memories around the senses—the smells, colors, or the feel of the weather at the particular season—but as soon as a face in the group lights up, he ceases giving his own memory and asks, "What is your memory?"

A co-leader may help, if no one else is yet ready, by quickly matching his memories with those of the leader. It sometimes takes a few moments for the process to get going. This part of the group conversation becomes a kind of weaving process, helped along, as the leader watches the faces, by such questions as these: "Is that like anything you did in your part of the country?" or, "Who has a similar memory, or even a contrasting one, for that, too, would be interesting?" The leader also holds in mind what he thinks might come next while a particular person is talking. Often it comes from the group. If it does not, the leader will be ready with his next pump-priming question.

After a few moments around the theme of the senses, the leader may ask: "What were we doing with other children, our brothers and sisters, or friends at school? What were the games we played?" It is amazing how easy it is to get grownups to revive those memories. If, at some point, the group seems to have strayed too far away from the topic, a co-leader can help pull it back with a memory more related to it.

If the leader senses that it is time to move on and someone is talking a bit too long, he can interrupt the speaker with a tactful question which would call for a short, direct answer, such as, "Was that your own experience?" or, "Is there a song you recall in connection with your experience?" Then feelings are not sacrificed, but the too long speaker will have been made conscious of the time. It is wise if, from time to time, the leader or a co-leader will give a quick, short summary or underline similarities in a casual way and, at the very end, make a final summary of what is significant. This should be kept simple. If someone other than the leader makes these observations spontaneously, so much the better. Be sure to keep a relaxed, though not a too slow, tempo. A sense of timing will tell when to move from one memory category to another.

To have no audience is very important, for even a few nonparticipating people in a far corner of the room detract from the mood of trust and acceptance and, hence, of spontaneity.

Participants enjoy not only recalling these childhood games and songs, but also reliving the experiences in pantomime. Once, a man from India was quickly on his knees with a man from Philadelphia, comparing how they used to play marbles in the spring. The leader would say, "Show us how you did it," or "Just give us an idea of how the song went—just one or two lines," or "Will you show us a bit of that Irish jig if we all clap the tune?" Don't wait for the answer, but begin the clapping. Remember that by now the powers of suggestion and imitation are strong. One of the co-leaders, good at folk dancing, is up beginning the dance, and others for whom it is a real childhood memory are now joining in. Sometimes, an elderly person will enjoy vicariously some dance learned in his youth, if others dance it. He may even dance a bit of the waltz or polka if the group hums a fitting melody. The leader and co-leaders can reach out for partners from the circle. Only a few minutes should be spent in this kind of activity. The leader, as soon as everyone is back in his chair, should quickly pick up the conversation thread as he leads into the next category of memories.

The involvement of the group in such action as folk games and dances should be made as natural as possible. There have been many successful experiences without such group movement, but it is psychologically valuable when it is included. When it comes, be sure that everyone is helped to participate in some way, perhaps by humming the tune (we can la-la-la in any language), or by the rhythmic clapping of hands while others dance. Co-leaders who are scattered in the group may be the first to start. As soon as the action is finished, everyone returns quickly to his seat, and the leader picks up the thread of the conversation. The artistry involved— and this will develop with practice—is to see that each part, individual memory of an event, song, or dance, flows freely into every other part without losing group attention.

Group recitations are also valuable in producing a feeling of unity. Those known and loved by several persons are especially effective. Sometimes a well-known poem such as "Trees," although it has been set to music, is rather difficult for a group to sing. However, it is excellent for group recitation. "The Night Before Christmas," the "Twenty-third Psalm," the "Gettysburg Address," "The Little Red Schoolhouse," are a few that have been used when they fitted into the topic and the mood. A few lines spoken together are sufficient. Attention should be directed toward the person who best remembers the lines so that recitation will be in unison.

Memories, Not Always Happy

A balancing of the contrasts in life—joy with sorrow, hope with fear, achievement with struggle—is a part of the art of group conversation. Sometimes, although not often, persons whose childhood had been particularly unhappy are present in the group. Some may remain silent, others may offer a sorrowful memory, which can bring the group into a deeper feeling of identity and acceptance. Still others may bring a note of bitterness.

When at a gathering Mrs. Smith in sharing spring memories said rather bitterly as she looked scornfully at the better-dressed women, "I don't have any pleasant memories. I always had to work," the leader answered brightly: "Yes, of course, work in the spring. Who also remembers work, good hard, satisfying work?" Several responded with pleasant work memories. The negative note was absorbed, and the feeling tone was changed, so as not to destroy the mood of the group. Mrs. Smith, however, may not have been greatly helped. She may have needed deeper therapy, and, if such were indicated, special help should be sought for her.

The sorrow note, on the other hand, is to be encouraged. In sharing experiences around the topic "Bread," for instance, we may give special invitation to someone who, as a child in Europe during a war, really experienced hunger, to share what that hunger meant. In one such case, someone pointed out that the hungering for love was even more devastating than hunger for food. The important thing was what the family did together in the midst of hunger.

In one situation there were two participants whose

homelands were then at war against each other. Each participant voiced his hatred of all people of his enemy country. The leader, who happened to be an American Negro, told how she had finally grown from hating all white people to using discrimination in her acceptance or nonacceptance of them. "It is easier to live with myself now."

We try to keep out of the conversation all spirit of competition. If, for instance, two persons belonging to the same faith began to differ as to the symbolic meaning of a certain festival, the leader can simply say: "All we want at this time is what you remember doing and feeling. Not all Christian homes do the same thing, nor do all Jewish homes, and yet we find there are amazing similarities in the midst of our diversity."

The Commitment or Ending

A certain amount of channeling is wise if the group is to arrive at any specific goals at the end. However, the leader should be alert to make the most out of what comes spontaneously in the group. He will soon realize that any cut-and-dried plans are as chaff in comparison to that which comes freely. One must be careful not to overpress the reticent person and yet give him plenty of opportunity to participate. This can be done by asking what was done in his part of the country or by a quick gesture of invitation around the circle just before moving into the serious ending. Asking if anyone has any special memory that has not yet been expressed will alleviate a sense of frustration. Many of the unexpressed memories will be shared between individuals during the refreshments.

Our psychiatric advisers tell us that amid the tensions of modern life, this act of recalling memories is extremely valuable for all of us. Moreover, the recollections serve to underpin a sense of commitment about the needs of the world today which can be stimulated in a skillfully handled group conversation. Unless one has spontaneous relationships of some kind that meet his personal need for expression, he is bound to have unsatisfactory relationships in his everyday life and in his business or work.[3]

The flow of the conversation must not stop abruptly just because the time is up. It is an experience that craves a significant ending. The leader, therefore, watches his time and allows at least five or ten minutes for the ending. If he has asked for memories of what was done in church, temple, or school, the symbolism of the season or of the topic will be touched upon in some memory. He picks up the serious note of that memory and suggests that the group conversation be brought to a close by looking at the deeper significance of the experience. He asks, not that there be discussion, but that as a group there be thinking along such lines as these: "What did we have in our youth that the world needs today?" or "Looking at the world as it is today, and thinking together as a group about our responsibility in meeting these needs, what do we as citizens in this community want to say to each other?"

Sometimes the mood is a quiet one. If so, the leader can suggest that "a few moments of silent thinking together might be good at this point." This period will not last long, but short statements of conviction usually come from the group. The leader can then ask if there is a serious song known to most which picks up the mood. It may, for example, be "America the Beautiful."

While the group is singing, the leader and co-leaders can reach for the hands of those next to them and rise. No words are necessary, for others will do likewise. This physical contact is psychologically valuable. Gordon Allport says that until we get this acceptance of others into our very muscles, glands, and bones, we do not really have it. Sometimes the group feels such a deep joy for having found a sense of kinship that some participants are on the verge of tears. We remember instances when in such circles there were remarks like this: "We could almost feel the prejudices dropping away."

If after a closing song the group feeling is very deep, there may be need for another and lighter song to release the group before going to refreshments. Or, a gay folkdance song which enables the group to go to and from the center of the room for a few moments with hands held high, and then breaking up with clapping, is an effective ending.

Often, when winter memories have been the

theme, groups express their feelings through a spontaneous, simple ceremony. Perhaps the lights are turned low, and the members are asked to light the various kinds of candles which have been explained previously. Thus, a Jewish person will light the *Hanukkah* candles, while the group sings the *Hanukkah* "Rock of Ages," which has been referred to during the matching of memories. If anyone has told about the Swedish St. Lucy's Day, that can be pantomimed, and finally a single tall candle can be lit for Christmas, while the group softly sings "Silent Night." In the ensuing silence, short significant statements will be made, and then a jolly song, such as "Deck the Halls," can be used to get the group to the place for refreshments in a lighter mood.

When the goal is mainly to become acquainted, the final act of the "social drama" is the party—which means anything included in its program that people find entertaining. Names and addresses may be exchanged. Announcements or decisions for a possible next meeting also may be made. The sharpness of this transition from the past to the present is essential to the real effectiveness of the whole performance. To relive the past, to enshrine it in memory and in art, to accept it willingly and cheerfully, and then to pass on in happy adjustment to the demands of the present—that is mental health both for the individual and for the group. It may help to produce more of that spiritual cohesion so necessary to our fragmented society today.

At the very end of the evening, a friendship circle can be formed. This brings the group together again while they sing the Scottish "Auld Lang Syne," or the Hawaiian "Aloha," or the Rotarian "The More We Get Together," or the very easy little song, "Make New Friends and Keep the Old, One Is Silver and the Other Is Gold," or the hymn, "Blest Be the Tie That Binds." Or, sometimes, while one person sings the words, the group hums an accompaniment. Some songs can be lined out—that is, the song leader quickly recites the next line while the group holds the last note of the previous line. This effective method of teaching a simple song—a custom we get from our southern Negro Americans—will have been tried out at the "planning meeting" by the co-leaders.

Some Caution Lights

This running description of how a group conversation grows from start to finish needs to be followed by a few important warnings that the leader should bear in mind:

Beware of:

. . . the too-long talker
. . . a willy-nilly conversation
. . . imposing a feeling of pressure to participate
. . . any spirit of competition or controversy
. . . encouraging a bitter note (Group conver-

sation is not group therapy, though the experience is oftentimes therapeutic.)

. . . poor timing by dwelling too long on any one category

. . . loss of attention, by being interrupted and distracted by latecomers, for example

. . . using any songs, statements, or terms not fully acceptable to all members of the group present; for example, telling any jokes at the expense of anyone else (We must remember that laughing *with* others unites, but that laughing *at* others separates.)

An additional word of caution is necessary about the use of terms, for it is easy for the novice to use the wrong one. Use words or phrases that give feelings of being included rather than excluded. Thus we say, "those of us of Negro background" or "those of us of Jewish or Christian faith." Never should a leader say, "you Jews" or "you Christians," or "you Negroes," or even "you people."

Do not expect all members of particular groups to be talented in the same way. Not all Negroes are able to dance or to sing well. There is a great variety of talent in every group. A few Negroes are still sensitive about the spirituals, though these are recognized the world over as great art. There seems to be a spiritual to fit almost every mood, and the right one often comes up to charge a group with a deep, meaningful feeling. But other people also know these songs; and so we need not look only to Negro participants to lead the group in singing them.

Americans whose ancestors have been here for several generations may be called "old-stock" or "old-line" Americans. But remember also that although these are mainly of British stock, many families of Spanish, French, Negro, and Jewish background may be also "old-stock" Americans, having been in this country for generations.

It is well to keep in mind that Puerto Ricans are American citizens, although they have a Spanish culture, and that Spanish is their mother tongue, as it is that of many people who have lived for generations in some of our states of the Southwest. Nor must it be forgotten that the Hawaiians and the Alaskans are bona fide Americans.

Unfortunately, the terms *interfaith, interracial,* and *intercultural* relations are often confused. The first has to do with relationships among people of various religions; the second, with the relationships among people of the racial groups (many anthropologists refer to only three major racial groups: Mongoloid, Caucasoid, and Negroid); the third term, *intercultural,* concerns relationships among all the various groups in American life, and could also refer to such groups on an international level. (The term *culture,* as used by most sociologists, refers to the typical ways of thinking or acting of a specific group of people.)

The Team Is Important

We have presented a picture of the structure of the group conversation itself. We shall look now at the necessary preparation before the actual conversation. In planning for the session, we suggest that the leader not work alone, but share at the beginning his interest with two or three others, so that a team may be developed. In this team, it is well that there be one who, having been a part of singing groups, knows the common songs; another who is familiar with the simple forms of group movement, such as circle dances; and perhaps a pianist who can play accompaniments on the spur of the moment.

These few interested people should meet for a preparation session. They might all belong to the same PTA, church, or social club, and be planning to gather a culturally mixed group under such auspices. Or, they might be three or four friends planning to start a group in one of their homes, in order to develop more neighborliness in the community. The situation determines the basic group to be invited, and how they should be invited. If people of different religious, racial, or national backgrounds are not now in the activities of the PTA, church, club or neighborhood, the leader may want to find ways to discover how to seek them out and include them.

In planning the session the leader would do well to use the following check list:

- Decide on time, place, refreshments, and focus of

beauty (flowers, or decorations appropriate to the occasion).

- Appoint someone to plan one or two name-mixing games for the beginning of the session (this is necessary only when most of the group are strangers).
- Choose the topic.
- Spend a little time recalling your own memories around the lead or pump-priming questions.
- Recall and try out songs that fit the topic.
- Try one or two simple group dances.
- Check list of guests—not more than twenty—or at least, until you have tried your hand at the method.

Sharing for a short while one's own memories spontaneously in the preparation session is in itself emotionally rewarding and gives the leader and his team an idea of what to expect in the later meeting. One or two ideas of what might evolve into a significant ending may also occur to the leader at this time. Several songs that fit the topic may be recalled. Singing out one verse and the chorus of each song could mean a lusty group-sing experience at the larger meeting. The same can be done for one or two simple group dances; for instance, "Oats, Peas, Beans," if the topic is to be "Bread." The group movement co-leader can be asked to be responsible for suggesting and leading the dance at the appropriate time, while the others readily co-operate, remembering that through the power of suggestion the whole group will easily follow. Most people enjoy participating in such simple dances if they are led well and if they fit into the mood of the group.

A word of warning belongs here: Although these preparation sessions are invaluable, the co-leaders should be told that spontaneity is of the essence. Hence they should not force into the later meeting memories which come in the preparation meeting, but should be sensitive to the mood of the group and see the group conversation as a new situation.

The Rewards of Research

During the period between the preparation session and the group conversation itself, the leader will want to look up material relating to the theme in Borland, Peattie, or similar books on the seasons, and in Spicer and Schauss on the customs of the groups that may be represented.[4] It is valuable for the leader to do some reading in comparative folk-lore and festivals. He must know beforehand if, for instance, the theme is early spring, that the mood of the Catholic *Carnivale* is similar to that of the Jewish *Purim*, and that both have their roots in the way our common dawn-age ancestors reacted to the change in the seasons. The leader need not feel he or she must remember these details. The guests themselves will give their own memories of what was done in their groups. The leader need only ask, for example, if there are Jews present, "Is there not a festival in the Jewish group at this season? Can someone for

whom it was a childhood memory tell us about it?"
If no one responds, then the subject is dropped. It
is not emotionally valid for anyone to report on such
an experience from simply having read about it.

We are now ready to think about the early phase
of the session. We should then first set the stage of
this theater in the round. The guests should sit in a
circle as close together as is comfortable, so that each
can see the other's face. The leader will sometimes
be in his seat and at other times he will be moving
in the middle of the circle (unless it is a small
group), the better to secure participation. In some
conspicuous place will be the focus of beauty, symbolic of the topic: flowers or fruits or candles indica-
tive of the season. If the gathering must be in a bare
schoolroom, union hall or gymnasium, it is helpful
to hang a colorful drapery on the wall.

Since most groups take about twenty minutes to
assemble, it is best to have an already functioning
social group into which they can immediately enter,
rather than to let them wait stiffly around for something to happen. If people are not familiar with each
other's names, it may be fun to have a name game
as an "icebreaker." The following game is often used:

The chairs are set so that the group arranges itself
in a circle. Members are introduced by what may be
called a "name game"—an interesting method of ty-
ing the group together by adding each new name to
the chain, all links of which are repeated for each
new addition. Thus, Jones, then Smith; the next is

Robowsky, and it continues: Jones, Smith, Robowsky, Peters, and so on, around the circle. When the chain is completed, each name has been repeated several times, and each individual learns by repetition the name of each other member. Be careful not to turn this into a memory test. Help each one to say the names when his turn comes. Incidentally, this device—hearing one's own voice and name several times—makes it easier for each to express himself, even the most timid.

When all the guests have arrived, the group conversation leader can take over by suggesting another game: "This is a game of matching memories." See that all are comfortably seated in the circle. One person should be appointed to meet any latecomers at the door, whisper a description of the game, and then ask them to sit on the floor cushions in the circle, if there are no vacant chairs. This makes for informality, and is done especially to keep the flow of group conversation from being stopped when chairs have to be shifted to enlarge the circle. Let nothing stop the flow of conversation, once it has started, until the hour is up.

When the Group Is Large

Group conversation is best for groups of twenty to forty, but sometimes, as in a Parents Association meeting, there may be need to accommodate from 300 to 400. We do not advise starting with such a number, but after some experience we find that it is possible to allow for some spontaneity in a large group and still handle the situation. First, there should be a planning session of fifteen or twenty persons who will represent the groups expected at the meeting, and who will act as co-leaders, scattered through the audience. A sample of memories will be matched, and songs and games recalled, during the planning session where the topic will be given a dry run. With such a large group it is best to seat them in concentric circles small enough so that participants can hear one another. The leader needs to be on his feet in the center throughout most of the session. He will find his own way to take away the formality of the meeting. For placing the people, he may ask for a show of hands of those who grew up in New England, the far West, the deep South, then coming back to the natives of the local community. "And if we are really lucky, we shall have people who grew up in other countries." Almost every American audience will have some persons of other nationalities.

In a large group, it is necessary to be certain that the suggested songs and dances are done well. A good pianist and song leader are invaluable and should function as co-leaders. If possible, secure the services of a professional folk singer and a folk dancer. These "stars" must, of course, weave their performances into the conversation in as spontaneous a way as possible. Acknowledgment or identification of these performers comes best at the end of the session.

For the ending, opportunity can be given for short expressions of conviction related to the topic. A community leader who has prestige for the group may be invited to sum up the comments and contributions of the meeting. Or the session may end simply with one or two appropriate songs, a jolly folk song and a circle dance at the last. It may also, particularly with professional artists, be brought to a more elaborate finale.

The Rewards of Follow-Up

The teamwork of leader and co-leaders should extend beyond the planning and conducting of the actual group conversation. They may wish to come together almost immediately afterward to evaluate what happened and to discuss plans for follow-up. They want to share with one another what they feel to have been the high points and to determine in what ways they fell short of accomplishing their aims. Although they have all had in this group conversation a common experience, each has seen the group process from a different angle. The interchange will be helpful in later experiences of this kind.

One of the co-leaders should have been asked to take notes of the group conversation just as inconspicuously as possible. Another co-leader may have been assigned to the job of group observer, watching the faces of the group members, noting those who participated and those who did not, and trying to sense why or why not there was participation. The observer also attempts to recognize the moments of group unity that may have been achieved and what was said or done that produced such unity. The situations in which the leader has failed to take advantage should also be noted, all these observations being made by a sensitive and understanding person whose only aim is to help this group of leaders to become more skilled in the art of group conversation. The co-leaders take turns in being group observers and, in the evaluation sessions, tactfully report their impressions as critics. During the period of informal socializing the team members will have heard comments of different group members and will have noted how certain persons reacted. All these reactions should be collected and put together in a report for the team of leaders or for the central planning committee of the ongoing project, if there is to be one.

The report will contain a running account of the group conversation. A complete stenographic record is not necessary, but the gist of each conversation is very valuable, especially if the report can be written by one who knows how to put it into a form that has objectivity, continuity, and something of the vitality and significance of what occurred. Not only should such a report be made available to those who attended the gathering, but it will be valuable for general interest, if it can be written so that the cultural richness and exciting variety in an otherwise drab community becomes evident. There are Americans who fail to see this diversity as a source either of strength or of conflict.

The nature of the follow-up will depend on the auspices under which the group conversation is held. If a particular institution sponsors it, such as a Parent-Teacher Association, a church young people's society, adult education classes, or a community center, then the session's follow-up can be a part of the regular responsibilities of the teacher or leader of such a group. In fact, it is quite likely that the leader or teacher's regular duties will be made easier, for interest is quickened, certain intergroup problems may begin to diminish, and creativity is released with the increased spirit of good will. Local leaders will realize that the use of group conversation is a part of an ongoing process of aiding individuals to believe in one another as persons, so that they will make the attempt to live together more harmoniously and productively, whether as families, communities, or nations.

We see, then, that we can think of group conversations as an art form, and of the leader as an artist, with all the humility an artist feels toward his work. Art is experience, and the task of the artist, be he painter, musician, or poet, is to take the unrelated elements of his medium and so organize them that they are in balance and harmony. The elements in this action painting are the individuals of the group. The leader tries to so use the spontaneity within the form of group conversation, that the reconciling spirit can break through the barriers which divide human beings.

A specialist in human relations [5] described his group conversation experience as "a sort of symphony. . . . A major theme ran through it, varied and accompanied by minor themes. Each section here, not strings and brass and percussion instruments, but the native American element—composed of many different races and cultures—made a harmonious pattern. . . . After such an experience, need people wonder just what it is that makes a united America?"

NOTES FOR CHAPTER 3

1. Matthew Miles, *Learning to Work in Groups* (New York: Bureau of Publications, Teachers College, Columbia University, 1959).
2. Reported in R. M. MacIver, *The More Perfect Union* (New York: The Macmillan Company, 1948), p. 285.
3. See Helen Jennings, *Leadership and Isolation*, 2nd edition (New York: Longmans, Green & Co., Inc., 1950).
4. See "Bibliography for Leaders" at end of book.
5. Bruno Lasker, in *Adult Leadership*, March, 1958, "Social Education Through Happy Memories."

4 : CONVERSATION TOPICS
FOR ALL GROUPS

For the purposes of group conversation there are three types of groups, and the leader must understand at the outset which kind he is to lead and with what goal in mind. Is it a group of people who represent different faiths or different nationalities, or different regions of the country, or even one that includes all these categories? Is it a homogeneous group, all of one faith, or one nationality, or one section of the country? Is it a group, either intercultural or homogeneous, that needs to focus on the individual so that self-understanding develops?

The needs that can be helped by the use of group conversation are, then, in these three areas: (1) *intergroup* understanding—by helping people of different national, religious, or regional backgrounds to see their cultural diversity as potentially and mutually enriching through awareness of their similarities; (2) *intragroup* relationships—by helping people within the same cultural group but of varying age, educational, professional, or economic experiences to accept one another and to enrich one another's life; (3) *intrapersonal* awareness, self-understanding —by helping individuals to know and accept themselves first in order to achieve the kinds of insight that will make not only for personal growth, but also for greater awareness of the needs of others.

The experience of a group conversation around any topic may affect any participating individual in any or all of these three areas, but we have found it helpful to use certain kinds of topics for each specific need.

FOR INTERGROUP UNDERSTANDING

One need not look hard for topics suitable to group conversations. They are everywhere around us. It is important, however, that the topic always have a universal appeal to which all members of the group can find some relation and to which they can respond. Moreover, the topic should in some way be related to group goals.

A group made up of people from culturally mixed backgrounds can be moved to an immediate feeling of relatedness to one another when they share their memories around a "seasonal" topic, because these experiences help them to see and feel the underlying unity of all mankind. The *intragroup* members, whether in the same or different cultures, achieve a feeling of unity more easily by sharing such experiences as those around memories of work, food, sense of time, schooldays, red-letter days. In the case of *intrapersonal* awareness, we have used questions on early family relationships, such as, Who punished us? How did we feel inferior to others? What gave us a sense of self-confidence? What experiences helped us to become less ego-centered?

Swift Roll the Seasons

Topics around the seasons which are especially good for culturally mixed groups, are outlined below. There is space to record here only a few of the seasonal customs most frequently found in the many hundreds of gatherings that have used group conversation. In some parts of our country there are Spanish-speaking Mexicans and Puerto Ricans, French-speaking Canadians, and our Indian Americans. Their memories will be very interesting. Then, too, with more than 60,000 foreign students now in the United States, there may be in our groups people from far-away places of Europe and Africa, the South Pacific, the Middle East, and Asia. In our group conversations they have always matched our memories with something similar in their own lands. Sometimes, of course, it is a contrasting element that lends interest.

As stated before, the leader needs to familiarize himself with customs of groups he thinks may be represented in a particular gathering. Books listed in the "Bibliography for Leaders" will be helpful. The leader himself will not describe the custom. He might, for instance, ask Jewish people: "Who remembers taking part in a *Sukkoth* festival?" Or, if someone from England or Europe is present, he may ask: "Who can tell us of the English Harvest Home or of the European St. Martin's Day?" Only personal memories are to be shared.

"Come, Ye Thankful People, Come!"

As the leader reads further in this area of seasonal customs and hears more people describe their memories, he will learn more of the basic similarities and will be able to point them up in the group conversation. For instance, sorrow and want, as well as joy, are expressed in the American Thanksgiving and in the Jewish *Sukkoth*. One-half of the Pilgrims had died during the first winter, and the wild turkey was almost their only food. The early Hebrews were wandering in the wilderness and had only temporary shelters in which to sleep.

Sometimes it is valuable to point out that a festival in one country may have been picked up and perhaps somewhat changed in another country. Our Halloween came from a combination of the English and Irish All Hallow's Eve, October 31, All Soul's Eve, November 1, and Guy Fawkes Day, November 5. All these the British have integrated into a week of masquerading and fun. In our country, the turning of "trick or treat" vandalism back into traditional thanksgiving, sharing with others, is an inspiration from UNICEF, and brings an opportunity and experience of international giving to the American school child today.

A thanksgiving theme common to autumn festivals will help the leader and co-leaders to make a summary about similarities and to use it in some way for a significant ending of a group conversation. These are the elements of similarity that can be emphasized:

- Appreciation of the beauty of nature.
- Joy expressed in thankfulness in the midst of plenty; or, if need be, in faith in the midst of want.
- The sorrow that accompanies the knowledge of the winter to come, and the joy of hope for the returning spring. "Everywhere in life, springtime comes after fall."
- The joy of sharing what we have with others, and the feeling of security that comes through group co-operation in the face of trouble or the coming of winter.
- The offering of gifts and caring for those in distress.
- The exhilaration in the face of cold, wind, and snow, that comes to people who are healthy in mind and body.

The Festival of Lights

When the topic is around winter themes, it is good to show that most cultures use candles or lights in some way—that probably they were used by our dawn-age forebears because of a constant fear of the darkness and anxiety caused by the slow return of the sun. The Scandinavians, especially the Swedish, observe St. Lucy's Day on December 13. The youngest daughter puts on a crown of greens with nine white candles, and serves coffee and cake to the family. Many Swedish churches in America still observe this custom. Jews light the *Hanukkah* candles, one each night for eight nights to celebrate the battle of the Maccabees, when right triumphed over might because of their trust in God. For Protestants and Catholics, Christmas commemorates the birth of Jesus, whose life demonstrated that love wins over hate. Here are some of the universal themes that can be used for summaries and meaningful endings:

- The fear that perhaps the cold and darkness will remain. Today this is symbolic, but none the less real, psychologically.
- The joy that comes when we realize anew that the "sun is returning, that the miracle is beginning," and that light and love are born again.
- The hope, as the light gradually increases, that the new year ahead will be better.
- The solemn dedication of ourselves to carry out in our lives that spirit of light, love, and faith in God.

"The Year's at the Spring"

The themes of the Christian *Carnivale*, Lent and Easter, the Hebrew *Purim* and Passover, and spring festivities all over the world can be called upon from the first of February through May. Because people have so many memories of these events, we have found it wise to use two themes: Early Spring, during February and March, which includes *Carnivale* and *Purim,* and Late Spring, during April and May, which embraces Easter and Passover traditions.

The underlying mood in all these celebrations of Early Spring is one of being tired of winter. The Chinese have their most joyous festival on their New Year in February. The Chinese Feast of Lanterns welcomes the return of spring after the dark winter months. And in March, on Ching Ming Day, they visit the graves of their ancestors, blending their reverence in honoring their dead with the spirit of a picnic in the fresh spring woods.

The Japanese celebrate February 3 as "Bean-Throwing Night," when all debts are cancelled. In March, there is the Girls' Doll Festival.

Most Americans, especially those who grew up in northern rural areas, will remember how they looked forward to ground-hog day on February 2, to see if spring would come early.

People from Christian countries remember February 2 as Candlemas Day, when candles are blessed in church, and they look forward to the joys of *Carnivale* before Lent, or the *Mardi Gras*. The Jews celebrate *Purim* in the same mood but it commemorates the downfall of the wicked Haman, as related in the

Book of Esther. Children act in plays, taking the roles of Queen Esther, Haman, and other characters in the Old Testament story.

Negro History Week was set aside to dramatize the contribution of the Negro to American life. It falls in the week of Lincoln's Birthday. Most cultural anthropologists agree that Negro Americans, having been for 300 years an integral part of our country, are not a distinct culture group. Except in a few isolated pockets, whatever distinctive memories they have are a part of the region in which they grew up. Negroes from the West Indies, however, are a distinct culture group, and leaders can expect from them memories that are interestingly different. Negroes from Africa, of course, are also distinct national culture groups.

These similarities in "Early Spring" festivities can be stressed:

- A sense of feeling tired of winter, and looking for the first signs of returning life, as we watch the struggle between winter and spring.
- The spirit of abandoned joy that comes when we know that spring finally wins in nature and in the hearts of men.
- The spirit of hope and of love which grows as life begins to return to earth.
- Cleansing and purification in preparation for the renewal of life.

- The making of plans for the work and activities ahead.
- The height of joy as new life actually bursts forth.
- Dedication to work still undone, and asking God's blessing on its fruition.
- Delight in the beauty of nature in the springtime.

Renewal and Rebirth

Easter and Passover, in the "Late Spring," dramatize the real magic of spring, the bursting forth of life after death. Easter celebrates the resurrection of Christ. Passover commemorates the release of the Jews from their bondage in Egypt under the leadership of Moses.

Early childhood memories of those born in the country will be of spring, flowers, freshly plowed ground, the singing of birds, and an actual bursting forth of our ten-year-old selves as we ran out to greet the spring. City children will have their special memories of the sounds, smells, colors of activities in the streets; and both city and country people will have memories of spring games. Only a word of suggestion is necessary for them to pantomime these games, as they compare, for instance, the rope-jumping jingles along the Volga with those of Philadelphia.

Memories of what we did as children during Easter will be of new clothes, special foods, egg hunts; and then the more deeply religious activities for Christians will be in taking part in sunrise services. "In Ireland, the very sun dances for joy," said one participant. On the continent, the church bells now "come back from Rome" to fill the air with their ringing. And what Californian does not, somewhere in his psyche at least, look for the swallows of San Juan Capistrano?

Jewish memories will be filled with the activities of preparation for the Passover meal: the symbolism of the egg and bitter herbs, the unleavened bread, the songs sung at the table, the youngest child asking the four questions, the mystery of Elijah's cup—all remind Jews of the goodness of the Lord in having helped them, centuries ago, to burst forth from slavery into freedom.

The Negro spiritual "Go Down, Moses" movingly picks up this mood. It acts as a bridge over which Jew and Christian can meet, not with words, but with the feeling that although our differences are both real and valuable, underneath our memories we know that it is the same Lord who enables us to emerge from winter into spring, from any kind of slavery into freedom, and from death to life eternal.

In April, the Japanese hold the Cherry Blossom Festival; and in May, the Boys' Carp-Flying Day. Even countries without winter have something special. For example, the year-round clemency of sunshiny Hawaii demands a dramatization of the greater luxuriance of spring. May 1 is the Festival of Lei, named in honor of the colorful garlands that are so much an expression of the island's floral splendor and spiritual warmth, when garlanded maidens sing "May Day Is Lei Day in Hawaii."

"And What Is So Rare?"

Memories of what we did in May, June, July, and August will be connected with confirmation in church and temple, May Day exercises, the last day of the school year, and then summer vacations with all sorts of picnics and camp memories.

The religious festivals will be connected with the Christian Pentecost, the Hebrew First Fruits of the Season (*Shuvuoth*), and the welcoming of the summer solstice in many lands. They have in common these themes:

- Joy in the "riotous excess" of nature at this time.
- A sense of security in the realization that the coming of the seasons will not fail.
- Thankfulness to God for the first fruits of the season.
- Sharing with others, and a feeling of sympathy toward the weak.
- A feeling of dedication to spread the spirit of brotherhood to the four corners of the globe.

These themes will be evident in the Pentecostal story of the gift of tongues and the Hebrews' reading of the Book of Ruth. These deep feelings of expansiveness to include all peoples seem to well up at this season from our realization that Mother Nature her-

self gives unstintingly of her energy at this time of
the year.

Let Freedom Ring

The freedom theme can be used at any time of the
year, but it is especially appropriate around the
Fourth of July, when freedom holidays in many
parts of the world may be recalled—like the French
Bastille Day, the Czech Jan Hus Day, and the Chinese Double Ten—for every nation has its special
freedom day and song. The Passover Feast is the
traditional freedom holiday of the Jews, and the recent creation of the Israeli nation may come in for
attention at our group conversation. The Negro
American is beginning to celebrate in January the
emancipation of the slaves by President Lincoln.

As with other topics, the memory sharing can begin with what we did in our families and in our
church or community groups, the special songs and
foods at picnics or other gatherings. There will be
commonly known verses or quotations on freedom
that lend themselves to group recitation. The oldsters and the youngsters can compare what was done
in the different generations; Fourth of July memories
of long ago can be amusing. The ending will bring
out the universal hunger of mankind for freedom
and our responsibility to cherish that flame. Only the
universality of the desire is stressed, for the unity of
the group must not be broken by a discussion of how

to preserve our freedom today. The leader must bear in mind, however, that such a consideration of freedom, and what action may be taken to safeguard it, may be important goals toward which the group conversation can lead, and so can be followed up at another time.

Sing Along the Way

Since only the songs which come spontaneously from the group are used, with the exception that once in a while an individual may be moved to sing alone a song known and loved by him, the leader and co-leaders need only be aware of the commonly known songs which fit the mood of a particular topic. Participants from abroad are, as a rule, only too happy to share their folk songs if we ask for them after we have shared our own. Of course, some members of the group may not have singing voices, but few will say "no" to an invitation to share "just a bit of the song to give us an idea."

It seems unnecessary to list songs for each seasonal topic, for they can be found in any good collection. People enjoy singing the songs they knew in their youth and, if most of the members present join in even a simple song like "Shine On, Harvest Moon," it helps to produce an underlying feeling of unity. The popularity of TV "Sing Along" programs proves the point. Even children are singing with grandparents such old songs as "In the Shade of the Old Apple Tree," "Down by the Old Mill Stream," "Go Tell

Aunt Rhody," "School Days, School Days," "Listen
to the Mocking Bird," and others of our more recognized folk songs. Be sure not to run a song down;
one stanza or the chorus is usually sufficient in a
group conversation.

Every nation or group has its freedom songs. The
Negro American has "Lift Every Voice and Sing,"
and "Go Down, Moses." The Jewish song of hope is
"Hatikva," now the national anthem of Israel. And
of course we all know the "Battle Hymn of the Re-
public," "Yankee Doodle," "Faith of Our Fathers,"
"America," and "The Star-Spangled Banner."

Leaders may wish to begin their own collection of
songbooks and perhaps of records. The books and
records are, of course, not to be used during the
group conversation. They can help the co-leader responsible for songs to recall the words and melody,
so that if necessary he can supply the words to the
group as they sing. Sometimes a participant will un-
expectedly give the words if he is encouraged. On
one occasion, when three students from Africa were
present, the group started to sing, but could not remember, the words of "My Grandfather's Clock."
One of the African girls had learned the song from
an English missionary, and so she lined out the song
for the group, to the surprise and delight of all.

Because most song collections carry only a few
spirituals, and because these songs are especially
valuable and easy for group singing, the following
list of some that have often been used is given:

"I'm So Glad Trouble Don't Last Always"
"How Did You Feel When You Came Out of
  the Wilderness"
"Go Tell It on the Mountain"
"Listen to the Lambs"
"Every Time I Feel the Spirit"
"You're Gonna Reap Just What You Sow"
"We Are Climbing Jacob's Ladder"
"Walk Together, Children"
"Put Your Hands on the Plow"

When leaders ask a group that is religiously minded to sing a song, they should be sensitive to the feelings of those of different religions. We know that certain terms, such as "Lord" and "God" are acceptable to both the Christian and the Jewish faiths, but that there are other terms or words which are used only by or for adherents of particular religions. A few winter festival songs acceptable by members of all faiths are "Jingle Bells," "Deck the Halls," "Oh, Tannenbaum," and "Here We Come A-Wassailing."

We have found that people of different religions do not mind listening appreciatively while those of other faiths sing their hymns, and some may even join in a song not a part of their faith; but they should not be required or urged by the leader to do so. When "Silent Night" is sung softly toward the end of a winter festival group conversation, after members of different faiths have shared their special songs of this season, such as "Rock of Ages" of the

Hanukkah, we have always found our Jewish friends participating in this most moving of the Christmas carols.

"Lully, Lully, Lullaby"

This is a good topic for a mixed group of mothers, especially mothers of young children, with a few grandmothers and other relatives present. Questions like why we choose particular names for our children, or how we were named by our parents, or descriptions of naming ceremonies, will bring out different culture patterns. Beneath will be seen the universal desire to dedicate the child to the good life.

The Old Testament story of Hannah and Samuel can be simply told as the group moves into an ending in which almost anything significant in relation to birth and early childhood education can be stressed. Think, for instance, of the symbolism in the theme, "Birth is the capacity to leave the old and to meet the new."

Mixed through the session, there will be a sharing of lullabies in different languages and group recitions such as "Where Did You Come From, Baby Dear?" as well as the humor of superstitions and old wives' tales of pregnancy and birth.

A meaningful ending may be suggested by Olive Shriner's *Dreams* in which fairies bring their wishes to the infant's christening. Participants may be encouraged to express their own good wishes for the new-born babies of the group—or of the world.

FOR INTRAGROUP RELATIONSHIPS

The more homogeneous groups in a community—churches, clubs, synagogues, single culture organizations—also have cause to bring their members into a deeper feeling of unity. Sometimes the need is to develop and bring to the group a common core of information and data on which to base decision or action about a task into which all must pool their resources and abilities. Sometimes what is indicated is down-the-line communication so that all may understand the reason for a decision or a program of action established at a higher administrative level.

Very often the need is more basic. What is called for may be what is sometimes referred to as group maintenance abilities, through which members may be helped to remove communication blocks and clear their feelings, one with another. This may be crucial to the life of the group.

Very often, also, this need is tied up with the larger cultural imperatives which everywhere loom up as needs in our society, disturbing our individual and collective consciences and challenging our equanimity, our feelings of security and adequacy.

"The Wisdom of Insecurity." In the face of inexorable and accelerated technological revolution and change, we are constantly confronted by choices to make, many for which we feel unprepared. Seeking security and acceptance, we make our decisions often by following along herd-fashion, conforming

blindly to patterns set by the bolder or more willful, or to those rising irrationally out of the generalized confusions and frustrations of a harassed people.[1] The security which comes from such conformity is illusory and destructive, we recognize; but we feel incompetent to do much else. Irritated by our inadequacy, we often become negatively critical of our leaders, and distrustful of our own judgment; yet we can find little comfort or confidence in the kind of anonymous authority which seems to dominate our actions or decisions today. We fall easy prey to headline machinations and advertising slogans and the robotic thinking and gadgetry existence that they impose.

Students of behavior, social scientists particularly, have yet to find evidence that there is not within any group the potential to resolve this rapidly spreading phenomenon in our society. Yet the drive toward sterile conformity and the distress that arises from it penetrate almost every aspect of human behavior and affect the quality and nature of our group relationships. The situation calls for our best efforts to explore and find the structures and processes necessary to ensure open communication and full use of our resources.

Living with Change. Many of us are hard put to decide whether we are for or against change, but we are in fact in the midst of inevitable and revolutionary change in every area of life today. To overlook this fact is to court disorientation. To face alone its disintegrating effects can be disastrous.

Through group conversation we can be helped by and with others, in a socially acceptable way, to share and compare our feelings related to these fragmenting experiences and be able to look at them in terms of today's challenges. The kind of reinforcement and support that can come from such exchange is not only reassuring in the face of the insecurity, but healing also. As Fromm [2] puts it, the psychic task which we can and must set for ourselves, is not necessarily a seeking always to be secure, but an ability to live in insecurity without panic or undue fear.

The group conversation leader, with certain insights in mind, can develop a pertinent topic toward an ending by which participants will be helped to see and feel that each shared insight operates in full measure for each person. As individuals and as a group, we can, in fact, begin to act on the insight and "partake in each other's having."

Toward Group Goals. It may be well then for us to look more closely at one topic, such as Work, and see several ways in which it can be channeled toward a particular need or goal or program. We should say again here that for the beginner it is easier to learn the simple structuring of group conversation if one first uses a topic around a season, especially if the group is culturally mixed.

Topics such as Work, Bread, School Days, Time,

Red-Letter Days, which can be used with mixed or homogeneous groups, we shall set up in a slightly different pattern in this section, because it will give the leader another way of looking at the development of a topic.

"The Lord Has Laid His Hand"

This topic dealing with work and rest after work has been used for several different goals, such as these: to prepare a group of community leaders later to discuss equal job opportunities; to inspire young people toward a more healthy attitude toward work so that they could enter into their lifework with a greater sense of dedication; to help the older members of a labor union to compare with younger members modern working conditions with those of a generation ago; to welcome some new refugees to a Rotarian luncheon; to help people from our North and our South to feel their common inheritance. In our Chicago story, told in Chapter 1, the reader will recall that this topic was used to help people become acquainted before discussing interracial housing in a suburb.

Introduction. The goal will determine what the leader will say in his introduction. After placing the group, he might ask for a memory of one's father or mother or of some older person doing some work in or about the house. Again, this brings in memories involving the physical senses which are particularly easy to draw upon and therefore good with which to start. The leader should put emphasis on "two or three sentences" and keep his own memory within that limit.

Developing the Topic. What was our first responsibility in the home, and how did we feel about it? After a few in the group have responded, the leader may ask: "What was the first work we did for which we got any pay? What did we do with the money? Did we share work with other members of the family? Is there a special feeling which comes from working as a team with others, as compared with working alone?" At this point the priming questions will be more closely related to the chosen goal whether it is toward the experience of working together in a labor union or toward choosing one's work in which a spirit of dedication can be developed.

Some pertinent questions to help a group think about their attitude toward work today are these: How do we feel when work is only a duty? Is work ever an obsession—that is, work for the sake of work? When do we feel like a cog in a machine? In our first jobs, did we feel closer to our fellow workers or to the customers? Did we converse with them? Is it possible to bring more human feeling into our work today?

If the topic is about our attitude toward a vocation, what is a vocation? A call, a sense of mission or concern? Is it the same kind of feeling as when members of nonreligious groups have a sense of dedication? (Do not allow discussion of this; merely ask the question.) If someone gives a moving experience of how he was led into his lifework, it can be meaningful to have the group or someone sing as a solo, the spiritual, "I Know the Lord Has Laid His Hands on Me." This experience can lead into the ending.

If the topic includes Rest After Work,[3] then the priming questions can lead toward Saturday night memories after the week's work and from there into ways of relaxing on the Sabbath.

The Ending. Almost any thread which may come in the sharing process and which seems important to the group can be developed into a significant ending. A short reading or recitation on "Work" from Gibran's *The Prophet* is impressive and fits any group. After this and a few moments of silent thinking, a walking circle can be formed as the group sings the spiritual "Walk Together, Children." The group is then released for refreshments and the party, if these have been planned. This type of ending may be omitted if the group is to enter directly into a discussion such as equal job opportunities.

The Little Red Schoolhouse

This is a good topic for any group, and one which can be geared to almost any group goal. If it is used with parents, it could lead them to want to go further in studying early childhood and its education; if it is a faculty group, it could sensitize them to some of their own and their pupils' emotional needs;[4] if an

international group, then it could help them to see
similarities and differences in educational methods.

Introduction. One will introduce the topic according to the situation and goals of the sponsoring
group. Then, "Shall we introduce ourselves and state
where we were at about the ages of eight to twelve
and, in no more than two or three sentences, give a
word picture of the schoolhouse as we remember it?
What color was it? Perhaps it is the room of our
favorite teacher that we remember." The group is
not far into a session usually before someone feels
like singing "School Days, School Days."

Developing the Topic. Questions like these may
be asked by the leader, only one or two at a time, of
course: "What do we remember doing with other
children? Did we help each other prepare our lessons? Did we compete for marks? How did we feel
about that? What were the games we played at re-
cess? What early friendships do we remember? What
teacher helped us most? Did any teacher block our
development? Did we ever move to a new school in
the middle of a school year? Were we then left out
of games? Were we rejected by other youngsters for
any reason? Were we ever the one to pull a lonely
child into the game? Was there some special event
in which we took part, such as reciting a poem, giving an oration, or acting in a play? How did we feel?"

The Ending. This will depend on what comes out
in the memories, and on the goals of the group. The
end can be focused on almost any pertinent need in

education. With the focus today on school integration in the North, as well as in the South, it is valuable to help dominant group parents become more sensitive to the feelings of minority group children. This can be done by having adults in mixed groups recall their own memories of rejection and acceptance in school or on the playground for any cause, and then ask the participants at the end of the group conversation to think together honestly about these conditions in their schools.

"Let Us Break Bread Together"

This is a theme of deep significance. It is easy to develop and it can be used for many different group goals. A need which is becoming better recognized by leaders of organizations working with young parents' groups is that of helping to build more significant family life. Psychologists are pointing to the need for families to revive or create new outstanding occasions for family observance.

Introduction. Perhaps the group has just eaten together or will be eating together. Almost any comment can start this topic. "Let's share our memories around bread and other food, and what our families did on special occasions around the table." The leader is careful when stating the topic not to choose too narrow a sector of experience. To use only the word "bread" may not lead the group on so well. This is important in stating any topic.

The focus of beauty can be samples of bread from different cultural groups, or one large loaf and perhaps a small sheaf of wheat on a front table.

Developing the Topic. Memories are elicited that involve first the physical senses—smells, taste, and so on. The leader's memory may well be that of smelling the freshly baked bread in his mother's kitchen, or going to a store to buy bread. It will help to ask questions that will lead to a few details: What shape was the loaf? What color? Do we recall one or two Mother Goose rhymes we were taught about food? (The entire group may recite together.)

Draw out memories of food experiences with other children: lunches at school, the cookie jar, refreshments at picnics. Dance games connected with food, such as "Oats, Peas, Beans" or "Jolly Miller" will help. Dancing or playing out a bit of some of these games can help to bring a group together quickly.

Memories of what we did and had in our homes (light and serious) at special meals of Thanksgiving, Christmas, Easter, Passover, and so on, or memories of different ways of saying grace can be summoned. The Orthodox Jews and the Catholics say grace both before and after meals. Quakers say grace in silence with bowed heads before meals. In some families grace is sung. If the group is mixed religiously, it is not wise to ask it to enter into the saying of grace. To tell about a way of saying grace is a quite different act. We never ask a religiously mixed group to end with a prayer or even silent prayer. To ask for group silence is not necessarily asking the members to join in prayer.

The Ending. The ending can focus on one of many themes: the hunger of the world and our responsibility to help, and the significance of the common meal for the family, are only two. If people of only one religion are present, the religious symbolism of bread according to their own custom can be appropriately stressed. If both Jews and Christians are present, some Catholic or Protestant who knows the subject may tell as simply as possible why the Catholic Mass and the Protestant Communion owe so much to Judaism. The spiritual "Let Us Break Bread Together on Our Knees" can be a very moving climax when such a theme comes up. It should be noted that often in what seems to be a culturally homogeneous group there may be several participants who will, in giving their memories, reveal their mixed backgrounds. In a suburban group of young married Unitarian couples, a Polish-American woman told of her family's still observing the breaking of the unleavened bread around the Christmas table. Three formerly Jewish women then showed from their memories a similar custom of the *Seder Mazoth;* and a second-generation Italian American and a Mexican American from El Paso were eager to tell of special things their family did around the table.

Red-Letter Days

This is a good topic to use with parents to encourage them to look critically at their own family traditions, or with teachers and others to help them acquire a fresh outlook on the emotional needs and behavior of children. Bossard and Boll discuss the importance of ritual for families today and emphasize aspects that may be suggestive to the leader.[5]

The Introduction. One may lead off with "Let's introduce ourselves around the circle clockwise, telling where we were at about eight to twelve in age and, in not more than two sentences, give our memory of the oldest person in our family at that time."

Developing the Topic. "There was a time when we all felt inferior in some way to these grownups. Perhaps a few of us can say what we felt inferior about. For instance, I felt I was ugly—my nose just too queer, and my hair too straight." Allow only a few examples of this kind of negative feeling, and then ask: "What events gave us a sense of self-confidence and of being accepted in terms of the grownups?" Evoke experiences like birthday parties, recitations at school or church, confirmations in church or temple, a first bicycle, a dress or suit for an important occasion, the first money we earned, a family anniversary.

How did our family give us a sense of belonging to a tightly knit group, or a sense of continuity with the past? Around this theme will cluster such memories as family gatherings at Thanksgiving, Christmas, Passover, and the like. What were the things the family did, or what was said by some adult that gave us this feeling of belonging?

When did we begin to understand that part of our own fulfillment was the effort to be unselfish, to help, to be less egocentric? A few memories will be of events in a church or a conference around a campfire at night, or what some inspiring older person said. Perhaps such a memory will be of something that happened on the football field, or even as one walked alone.

The Ending. A fruitful ending for such a topic is to ask, not for discussion, but for a few statements related to how young people today can be helped to use their red-letter events for personality growth. Often a group of parents will ask themselves if they are providing for their children the kind of settings in terms of today's needs that will be emotionally satisfying. The group can then or later decide whether they want to follow this group conversation with any kind of ongoing activity.

"A Thousand Years Are But a Day"

Group conversation can be used to help older folk do more creatively what they enjoy doing anyway, that is, to reminisce. It is also an effective way to prepare a group for participation the following hour in a discussion of some aspect of gerontology, with a resource person giving some factual material on the subject. Various topics may be used, of course, but a specially good one is Growth.

The Introduction. The leader might say that since modern psychology is telling us that personality growth need never stop, it might be valuable to go back to share our memories of our own physical, mental, and spiritual or psychological areas of growth. Then the participants are placed as to where they were at the ages of eight to twelve, and are asked to give in one or two sentences a picture of their house—was it in a city, a town, or on a farm?

Developing the Topic. Such questions as these may serve to draw out the group: "Do we remember wanting to grow up very fast? Did we mark our height on the wall once a year? Did our grandparents or other older people give us folklore or superstitions related to growth? (Do you remember 'Whistling girls and growing sheep are the most profitable things a farmer can keep'?) What accomplishments marked the highest moment of our physical growth? Did we compete for marks in school? What teacher or experiences, in school or out, helped us most to grow mentally? What was our most significant moment of social acceptance at what age? Was it at graduation time? What were some of our first wonderings about life, such as time, stars, God? Does anyone want to give a short statement of his faith today? Perhaps the words of a great poet or prophet will express what you would like to share."

The Ending. The leader might state that the Over-streets say we need never stop learning, loving, wondering, creating, and communicating. According to them, these are the five inexhaustibles. If a few young people are present some older person may be inspired to say what he feels is the most important bit of wisdom he has learned in life.

Yesterday Is Today's Memory

There are many deeply meaningful memories as well as entertaining experiences which may be developed around the topic of Time, in any kind of group at any time of the year. Of course, it fits especially at the New Year season. Sophisticated participants will share deep philosophical ideas, and youth groups will receive stimulation for thinking out their own philosophy, especially if a few "wise" adults are present. It is good also if two or three Oriental or South American or African guests are present, for they may be from cultures with a different sense of time from ours.

The Introduction. The leader might introduce the topic by referring to our feeling of not having time enough to do all the things we want to do.

"What was our earliest feeling about time? May we go around the circle telling where we were at the ages of eight to twelve, and describe in no more than two or three sentences the memory of a clock that comes back to us?" The song "My Grandfather's Clock" usually evokes many a picture of a clock on the stairs.

Developing the Topic. How did we first learn to tell time? What kind of person taught us? Did we have a sense of mystery in connection with the concept of time, of the seasons, of space? What jingles did we learn like "Thirty days hath September"? What childhood verses, like "In the winter I get up at night/ And dress by yellow candlelight./ In summer quite the other way/ I have to go to bed by day."

What celebrations or events marked the passage of time—of night and day, of summer and winter; birthdays, New Year's Day, and other seasonal events? (Not all these need to be used in one session.)

What is psychological time? When is time short, and when is it long? Time as experienced by the very young, and by the very old? "One day is with the Lord a thousand years. . . ."

The Ending. The possible endings will be as varied as the interests and needs of the participants. What is the meaning of "I do not have time" in our age of time-saving devices? If anyone is present from a culture which does not have our feeling about the importance of many activities, and of being on time at each of them, it would be good to compare these values.

Cold Blow the Blasts

To share experiences of storms is another fruitful source not only for group entertainment, but for recognizing our closeness to the elements. Sometimes tragic or near-tragic experiences will be shared.

The Introduction. After placing the group members, the leader can begin by asking for memories of "our family in a storm, or during a cold winter evening, when we were eight or ten." Described also will be the stoves around which we sat, the snacks we ate, the songs we sang, the family games; and some will remember the family prayers, just before going to bed.

Some of the oldsters will remember the Saturday night bath, taken in the winter behind the kitchen range. Some of the group will be willing to dance "Here We Go, Looby Loo," that lively bit of Americana, which commemorates the weekly splash in the family tub.

Development of the Topic. Outstanding incidents of special storms or floods may be shared and will determine the type of ending. Perhaps it will be the surprising sense of unity which can come to strangers who experience a storm together. The question of how this sense of unity can be stimulated in community life without waiting for a storm might be asked. What can we in this community do to help us face the future with more courage? This need was pointed up by President Kennedy, in his Chapel Hill speech of October 12, 1961: "We are destined, all of us here today, to live out most, if not all, of our lives in uncertainty, challenge, and peril."

The Ending. The ending note will depend on what significant ideas have come out in the session. There is, for instance, the importance of doing things together in our families, and in smaller groups of friends, which give both young and old such a deep sense of continuity with the past and of security in the present that they can face the storms of the future with more courage.

Life as a Journey

This is a valuable topic for youth or age, or both together.

The Introduction. The placing can be, along with their names, a two-sentence description of the place in which the participants grew up—farm, small town, or city.

Developing the Topic. "What is our earliest recollection of a road or a street? What time of the year is it, and do we see anything moving? What early journey with our family comes back to us? Is it the journey or the arrival that comes back to us more vividly? What was our first trip alone? Did any of us ever run away from home, or plan to do so? What trip became the most significant in that it deeply influenced our lives?"

The Ending. This will depend on the nature and goal of the group. Religious groups will move naturally into symbols and meanings significant for them. One emphasis on which Americans in general might end the group conversation, is the idea that we all have pioneer blood in our veins. In this space age, what are some of the new dimensions in individual, family, and community life that we should be mapping out?

Other Topics May Be Used. The reader will see that a great variety of topics may be used: What Books Have Meant to Me, Animals I Have Lived With, My Most Creative Moment, Ways I Have for Communicating with Others—to mention only a few. Care should be taken not to take too small a section of a subject. Instead of Trees, for example, more can be developed out of On Being Close to Nature.

Because the emphasis of the third category of group conversations, as set forth at the beginning of this chapter, is focused on the *individual* member, and only indirectly on the group as a whole, it is approached in a manner different from the first two which we have just discussed. The preparation and understanding that will enable the leader to help the individual member to understand himself are developed in the following chapter.

NOTES FOR CHAPTER 4

1. Our extreme concern over bomb shelters and fall-out and the impact this concern can make on family life is only one aspect of our general sense of insecurity. How close the problem of fall-out is with us may be seen in the moving report of one mother in a group conversation. Her children expressed such distress,

after a discussion in a school science club meeting, that never again could they safely have fresh snow-cream in the winter.

2. Erich Fromm, *The Sane Society* (New York: Rinehart & Co., Inc., 1955).

3. For material suggestive for developing this and other topics, if the goal is to help overcome barriers between North and South, see James McBride Dabbs, *The Southern Heritage* (New York: Albert A. Knopf, Inc., 1958).

4. Arthur T. Jersild (*op. cit.*) has suggestions which a leader can use for questions related to this need.

5. J. H. S. Bossard and E. S. Boll, *Ritual in Family Living* (Philadelphia: University of Pennsylvania Press, 1950).

5 : SELF-UNDERSTANDING— THE LIFE DYNAMIC

It was the need for finding ways of helping people of diverse backgrounds to communicate and relate to one another that the group conversation method was developed. Its focus on the person soon revealed its value as a process for meeting certain intragroup and intrapersonal needs of participants as well. Culture and culture-related experiences carry our individual emotions. When they are shared in a relaxed, trustful exchange, they can open up other areas of involvement and inquiry. In the context of the group we may be stimulated to identify and clarify problems and pressures which have been teasing and haunting us just below the threshold of consciousness—only, however, if we feel we have the support and strength of the group.

The Individual Is Central to the Group

As society becomes more complex, we find ourselves being a part of more and more kinds of groups and situations with more and more kinds of people.

We also develop a greater need to establish our uniqueness as persons and to affirm our identity. As we better perceive the many and complicating obligations we need to fulfill from day to day, we see increasingly the urgency that we function as whole persons. Unless we are able to maintain a degree of stability and get some sense of center, playing out each of the many roles demanded of us can be a very fragmenting process. Pressured and torn apart by our many involvements and problems, few of us achieve this level of personhood, wholeness, and inner poise.

Too often we are captive to inhibitions born of a mistrust of ourselves or others, and of a preoccupation with what we feel they expect of us. The tension which is built up in each encounter is multiplied by the many situations of which we are a part, and intensified by similar pressures operating on other persons with whom we make contact. The strain of belonging increases with each group into which we come; and we may find ourselves more separate, more splintered, as we seek the harder to belong. A sense of futility follows upon the feeling of fragmentation. Life seems to have lost meaning because as we work to find or to be a part of everyone else's life-frame of reference we lose our own bearings, and deny our own values which nurture our being and spirit.

Very often the sense of separation is of a deeper, more remote origin. Psychologists give increasing importance to the relations between certain early experiences and mental health. Childhood conflicts can leave emotional scars whose psychological components may be so damaging and lasting that inability to resolve them or to integrate them into the ongoing encounter, may indeed set up serious road blocks to our continuing growth. Traumatic experiences are not, of course, confined to childhood. Many events befall us from time to time which either take their toll or help us to grow.

The Child Is Father to the Man

Memories of early events and their emotional color are central to certain phases of group conversation. Whether or not we are conscious of their impingement on our psyche, the quickening that comes with the recollection gives testimony to their meaningful content. The excitement is a genuine sentiment, and its fullness reaches out to others.

In creating a setting where the participant is helped to speak from his experience and his feelings, a well-led group conversation can encourage even the shy or inhibited person to test his data on himself and his group. In the telling he will find that his recollection of an event memorable to him becomes invested with all the excitement or poignancy of the encounter. He is the child again, and his listeners go to his experience with the openness with which adults receive the grace of a child's emotions, his gift. And because it is a child's experience, responsibility for its negative components, if such there are, need not devolve upon him. He can then come to the experience in its validity, its wholeness. The following will illustrate:

"I don't think I was quite seven. My mother's skirt was very wide but not wide enough to protect me from the thundering bellow of the white policeman's voice or the deafening blast of his gun. Nor was it wide enough to shut from my eyes the horror of my Rex's pain as he lurched and dropped writhing to the ground. 'This will teach you black buzzards to keep your dogs from white folks' flowerbeds. And this will teach you never to contradict a white man, let alone an officer again.' And with that, he fired another shot into my collie, as my mother protested again that Rex had, only a few minutes ago, come back with me from several days at my grandmother's, and could not possibly have been responsible. It was many years before I really felt I could speak honestly with a white person or get anywhere near a white policeman again."

Seen in wholeness, even a difficult episode becomes tenable. In receiving it again into our lives in the perspective of a good group experience, the individual is helped to accept his involvement in it, and a little more of himself in the bargain. In an atmosphere of compassionate give-and-take, the encounter acquires larger human dimensions, and each person can take sustenance from it and grow. One participant in a group series wrote: "In this listening-to-self atmosphere . . . I hear this in myself: an apologetic note; a fear that I will be rejected. I am aware. I can try to change."

The Grace of the Unexpected

In few of our daily experiences, circumscribed as they are by social restraints and inhibitions, do we feel free today to laugh at the unexpected or to cry out at the poignant. We are as blocked about exclaiming at the joyous wonderment about us as we are of forgiving ourselves and others for shortcomings and transgressions that can be made important to our development. By helping participants to share experiences of this depth in a climate of acceptance and trust, a psychological need, which it may be difficult to fulfill in another setting, may be met by group conversation.

It is easy in the sophistication of electronic brains, teaching machines, and interplanetary rockets to minimize this need for human fellowship. It is need for a kind of sharing that helps to overcome our fears of one another and an undifferentiated tangle of anxieties in a world shot through with fears and anxieties.

We have come to know, for example, that it is the tense and irritable business man who is susceptible to peptic ulcers. It is the tired, overwrought mother who can easily fuss herself into a nervous breakdown. The emotionally insecure and fearful child may soon cross over into delinquency or illness. Each person exhibits a need to know the comfort of another human ear or the understanding of a fellow being.

Group conversation does not look to work principally with the psychologically crippled person, ill with deep and serious conflicts. That is the province of the psychotherapist. However, for most of us, it can bring forward experiences which have important emotional reference. Their sharing can give creative release, and, like all creative experiences, has therapeutic effect.

Know Thyself

As teachers or leaders we are made constantly aware of the need to understand subsurface factors which underlie the behavior and actions of persons with whom we work and to relate these elements to impinging social forces. We must know, too, that a prior requisite is insight into our own drives and needs. Why, for example, do we choose a vocation or a group role which often places us in a position of leadership and dominance? Why do we feel the compulsion or responsibility to maintain certain patterns of conformity or convention in our group relationships? In a group conversation, a participant was stimulated to query, "As for myself, I have been asking, Why am I in my present job of being responsible for better race relations within the church? Is it because I feel threatened within myself and because of my difficulty in identifying with others?"

Much material of this nature is accessible through

skillful use of group conversation. In small, close groups, a series of sessions may be structured around certain early events in the family, the playground, the schoolroom, and the neighborhood which may have important current implications. Sharing in such areas of experience and impact as patterns of authority, peer relations, feelings of adequacy or inadequacy in terms of operations defined by adult dimensions, can make for deeper psychological penetration and draw forward experiences which, in the sharing, can result in insight and critical analysis.

If the leader is adept at bringing out and building on the feeling quality associated with these red-letter happenings, then matching memories around events which stand out as having made us feel important, such as birthday parties, winning school or athletic honors, confirmation services, and the like, can help to reaffirm and reinforce a sense of identity and roots. We can go from the security of this level of sharing to ways in which we felt inferior and inadequate. Some of us may have been ashamed of a too large nose or of picket-fence legs, of too much fat or too little hair, or too dark skin; of foreign parents who have difficulty making their verbs or their "th's" behave, or of home-grown folks with serious pocketbook problems. We may have been made to feel less than ourselves because we lived across the tracks or on a farm, or in a slum basement.

How did we overcome these feelings of inferiority or did we? We may reach back for experiences and feelings of rejection as well as of the security of belonging. Along with these can come recognition of our own rejection of other individuals or cultures or family patterns. In examining these experiences as a group, we can gain insight into those aspects of our own behavior as leaders and teachers which may keep us from being as effective in our work as we might otherwise be.

From a participant responsible for a large national professional and lay leadership training program came this evaluation: "My feelings which came up during the group conversation were negative and unhappy ones. I could allow them to come up perhaps because I was not responsible for leading the group or for creating the atmosphere as I usually am. I could follow my feelings, and now I see that I am more in touch with my unhappy feelings than with my creative ones. Perhaps I have repressed them in the past."

We can also achieve a greater degree of understanding and acceptance of the behavior of co-workers and fellow beings. On several occasions we have found that the sharing has helped to bring more rapport between dominant and minority groups, as well as among the members of any one of the many groups that are a part of American society.

How deep the response can be may be seen in the following comment from one participant about another in one such session: "Her face as she told of her childhood experiences at the Passover *Seder* was almost transfigured, as though she was reaching for this memory not back in her own lifetime only, nor even that of her cultural group, but into the memories of the origin of the human spirit."

On another occasion, one was moved to speak from the depth of a kindred emotion: "It is so hard when you don't belong. I remember when I was twelve, and we had moved into a new neighborhood. The fellows would lay for me, time and again, and beat me up because they could not stand a white Negro. I felt so bad and would sit for long hours in the sun. But no matter how hard I tried, I could not get my skin dark enough."

The quiet voice of the man and his simple dignity of manner did not completely mask the boyhood torment he was reliving. The thoughtful silence that followed showed how deeply his listeners were pursuing the intricacies of their own feelings, or reflecting on the devious twists of human fate when the heart is poisoned by resentment and prejudice.

Leaders in the field of human relations are becoming more aware of the close connection between mental ill health and prejudice. Gordon Allport says that prejudice is a "psychological crutch for persons crippled in their encounters with life." [1] We know that also it is the unhealthy mind that hates its neighbor.

Race Prejudice as Self-Rejection

Laurens van der Post speaks of race prejudice as a

form of self-rejection. The individual who cannot accept himself cannot accept another, and projects his hatred and fear of certain aspects of his own nature onto others.[2]

Much of the problem of self-acceptance or lack of it on the part of millions of minority-group people in American life is related to the varying degrees of prejudice on the part of dominant groups. Parents of minority-group children are often at a loss to know the best educational process to develop self-acceptance on the part of their own children. When a Southern mother has to choose between sending her child to the circus on the one day set apart for Negro youngsters or, on principle, keep him away from the performances altogether, she finds it difficult to explain either decision to the satisfaction or comprehension of his young mind. Yet it is experiences like these and others more violent in expression, that bring shame to the young heart who early learns to reject his people, his family, himself.

Social observers are warning us about the dangers of too much conformity in our community life. Psychologists tell us that it is not healthy for people with emotional roots deep in the cultures from which they or their recent forebears have come, to cut themselves off completely from these roots. Psychological research is insistent about the correlation between childhood experiences and adult personality structure.

The denial to a person of this right to be himself,

the most common manifestation of prejudice and intolerance, often makes some of our people shy or sullen; a few, aggressive or defiant. "To have loved is to know how to love; and to love and be loved is to be hopeful about life and most of the people one meets during the course of it," [3] is a positive corollary to the foregoing truism.

Could our present high delinquency rate and sterile conformity be partly due to this sense of rejection on the part of millions of Americans—a sense of inferiority fostered in culturally and economically deprived home circumstances, not adequately counteracted in church, school, or community life?

Venture in Depth

If we can, in a group, be helped to look at some of these kinds of subsurface data, which, in some degree, are a part of all of us, we may be supported in our efforts to break through to more creative use of our resources and talents, and to a deeper relating to other people, to life.

"The greatest failing of our time," writes van der Post, "is disobedience to our own greater awareness of life. A person who is individual in the contemporary sense of the word, is someone who always strives to make the universal specific, the general particular, the unconscious conscious, and the collective, individual." [4]

How to point up this deeper disobedience to our own awareness of being, would seem particularly important to those of us who accept responsibility of leadership. If we can explore and better understand the affective roots of our behavior and attitude, we may better recognize the emotional undertow that sometimes endangers the relationships we may have with others.

The leader who has good grounding in psychological principles and practices, or to whom the resources of a psychotherapist are available, would find it rewarding to try using group conversation at this deeper level. The process of inreaching for early experiences of emotional moment is the same, but the sharing will be around events in terms of a sense of recognition and importance or the trauma of rejection in relationships with adults and peers. The leader will find that as he develops confidence in the process and the group, he can plumb for deeper and deeper data.

Inreach for Outreach

In small experimental groups, the Workshop for Cultural Democracy sometimes brings together men and women in a co-operative search for this kind of growth and emotional maturity. These inreaches for meaning and wholeness are conducted with professional psychological guidance and are oriented toward creative unfolding rather than therapy. They run for ten to twenty four-hour sessions. The group conversations are paralleled by other projective or expressive instruments such as psychodrama, creative fantasy, dream analysis, and special applications of the graphic, plastic, movement, music, and writing arts.

Participants share experience and feeling, idea and image as these impinge on the life fabric of love, hate, joy, grief, ecstasy, pain, hostility, anxiety, siblinghood, friendship, parenthood, matrimony, sex identification, authority relationship, social rejection and prejudice, work attitudes and responsibility patterns, religious orientation, and spiritual motivation and response. Archetype, myth, symbol, and other psychological constructs, set in dynamic against these raw data, help to bring out new experience and insight, fresh energy and resource, expanded dimension and perspective.

In a painting session which had followed a group conversation around self-images, a participant in one such series surprised herself with a self-portrait which resembled a streetwalker. "I guess this shows that my neighbor *is* myself in the deepest sense only when we realize that in the unconscious levels of our being, we are organically one—in that sense, as long as another is in prison, I am in jail and with all streetwalkers."

Group conversation seeks, therefore, to fill a need for more effective ways to counter the feeling of isolation, rejection, and separation that seems to increase with automation, mechanization, and urbanization. It aims to reach deeper layers of the spirit so that we may be helped to a new or renewed sense of human community and dignity of person.

By investing each member of a group with a sense of his particular worth, it seeks to bring back into the group the primacy and importance of the individual, whose needs are too often sacrificed to the purpose and demands of the group. This does not deny in any way the significance of the goals of the group. Rather, it emphasizes the need to find ways to bring into the life and work of the group the full energy, talent, and commitment of all its members.

We live in human society and perhaps optimally function in a climate of security and trust, and in a recognition of mutual need and service. Group conversation aims at developing this feeling of mutuality and community. Underpinning its dynamics and philosophy is the democratic concept which all Americans should share.

NOTES FOR CHAPTER 5

1. Gordon W. Allport, *The Nature of Prejudice* (New York: Doubleday Anchor Book, paperback, 1958).
2. Laurens van der Post, *Race Prejudices as Self-Rejection* (New York: Workshop for Cultural Democracy, 1956).
3. Selma Hirsch, *The Fears Men Live By* (New York: Harper & Brothers, 1955), p. 115.
4. Laurens van der Post (*op. cit.*)

6 : RELATION TO OTHER GROUP METHODS

Very often a group conversation stands as a complete program or session, and in itself can be an aesthetic and satisfying social experience. Members of a group can be helped to have a sense of being part of a unity greater than themselves, yet feel a wholeness in and of themselves. This is to say that a group conversation may be used simply to give an aggregate of persons a chance to share in a common experience of coming together on a level of fellowship that can be highly rewarding and sustaining. A recent participant wrote: "I had a vision of happiness—perhaps for the first time in my life. . . . I think it is because of the feeling of true fellowship."

An Experience in Groupness

However, the group may have other goals toward which coming together on this dimension can be a productive first step. Organizational or community aims may look to constructive action about particular problems or to a deeper study of social issues or civic concerns. Here group conversation is used to develop the rapport that can help the group to absorb and resolve pressures and tensions that may ensue. Issues and problems have sides, and sides have a way of growing into conflict unless we are willing and able to *listen* creatively, and with patience, understanding, compassion, and objectivity. This calls for trust and confidence and, equally important, the feeling that this is our problem; it is of us all.

Many group leaders have described ways of helping participants to get the most out of the discussion phase in a problem-solving process. It is not often recognized, however, that there is also need for more ways of first freeing us of the kinds of blockages which keep us from getting the best results in discussions.

We are all too familiar with the kind of bogging down which brings many a meeting period to a disintegrated, distraught, frustrating, and inconclusive close. Time and energy for discussion are consumed in not very relevant disputation, and with the session's end closing in on the group, frantic but necessary decisions often get left to only a conscientious few. They are forced to take over a responsibility which belongs to the whole group, then find it next to impossible to get the membership to join them in carrying out needed decisions.

It is difficult to overstate the value and the strategic impact of this kind of sharing when we are looking for commitment and constructive action on group or community problems. Generally we are moved to act with others only when we have participated in the making of a decision in which we have been personally and emotionally involved.

As has been shown, the blockages, the conflicts, the difficulties, may be a matter of age or interest levels, status, or newness to a group or work situation. The barriers to communication are legion and as wide as life itself. As leaders, we must be sensitive to them. We must be sensitive, too, to the feelings of those who are caught in them. One of the most important ways of developing this kind of sensitivity is to become more aware of our own feelings of need and insecurity, to acknowledge and understand them. If we can, and do, set up the kind of situation where we can share these feelings and explore together their implications, we can more effectively function as leaders and group participants.

If we are mindful at the outset to take care of some of the personality needs with which most of us come to any new problem or group situation, we can better keep to a minimum their breaking out at more crucial times, to distort, divert, and dissipate considerations that need our complete, honest, and dispassionate attention and faculties.

This implies that the group conversation can lead to further steps in the process of working on a group's concerns, and calls for the use of other processes which can be incorporated with the group conversation.

Group Discussion Built on Groupness

Perhaps the most natural combination is with group discussion. If we assume that a group goes from discussion to problem solving and decision, thence to commitment and action, then group conversation may be seen as a prior step to this progression. Group conversation prepares for profitable discussion by helping to point up the basic and strategic aspects of a problem so that the group can look squarely at what is the issue, then get to work on it. Too often we cover up what is fundamental by cluttering the issue with nonessentials; we lose sight of the goals of a program or the crux of a problem. We consciously and purposely hide certain crucial data from others, or unconsciously secrete them from ourselves. Here is where group conversation can be especially helpful; it can bring up to the level of awareness much of the material that our very rationalizations either as individuals or as a group have pushed below.

Sharing earlier experiences of having been made to feel strange or different or queer, or occasions of being rejected or rejecting, for example, may bring important facets and depth to the exploration of some aspect of the fair employment or school integration issues. The kind of data we should need to look for, how we could best go about getting at them—in fact, the very way we formulate a problem —could be uncovered by the kind of interchange at this level of emotional involvement.

The discussion phase may flow directly out of concerns pointed up in the group conversation and become one continuous process if the leader feels at home in both techniques. Or, the discussion may follow a coffee or refreshment break.

Often it is wise to leave the discussion phase to another person skilled in its use. Especially is this so, if the group is large and the group conversation has been a particularly moving experience. The situation calls for a shift of psychological gears, so to speak, a change which is sometimes difficult for one leader to make. We shall find the group not only able, but very ready, to get into the thick of the discussion, and with a more open frame of heart and mind. A busy industrial leader, given a chance to reminisce on his early rivalry with an older brother, may suddenly be helped to see the need for along-the-line decision making in his factory work situation. A teacher recalling an early unfortunate classroom encounter in her first term as a student, may be made more sensitive to the needs of her incoming pupils.

Though it is most often easier and more natural to get into the discussion phase when the group conversation topic has been carefully selected to lead into the subject of the discussion, it can be said of group conversation that if it is a well-developed and skillfully led one, almost any topic can be used to open up a group to its next step. However, best results come where some real thought has gone into the choice of the topic and its structuring. If we are mindful to allow for real spontaneity, the flow into the discussion can be very smooth, and much of the relaxed climate and *esprit de corps* generated in group conversation can be carried over.

An Impetus to Conference Progress

For introducing the theme of a conference, seminar, or workshop, group conversation can be very effective. It can help a group, meeting for the first time, and for such a short period, to move into the matter at hand much more rapidly and directly. Not only can the necessary details of introduction be taken care of, but attendant anxieties to establish identity and "protocol" (a need so much more pronounced in the frenzy and briefness of conference encounters), can be allayed. Members are more ready to "buckle down" to business, but at a depth so as to proceed with intensity and progress. Many leaders who have worked a group conversation into the schedule find that the time is more than compensated for by the speed with which the rest of the meeting moves into the heart of the discussion and action.

There may be occasion to use several group methods with group conversation. We assume here that most group leaders are familiar with the methods we shall discuss here. As an initial event on any program, group conversation can be valuable for the reasons given above. It may be used at any time in a schedule to open up a session, or a discussion, or a new structuring of the group.

If the assembly is a large one, the different units may be set up in a concurrent round of group conversations. A skilled leader can work with a very large group, but should not look for as deep penetration in the individual experiences. Through vicarious participation, however, a group mood can be developed even in a large gathering which carries over into other parts of the program. If the conference is on urban renewal and housing, for example, a group conversation carefully planned to elicit emotionally contentful experiences around home or rooms with which we can identify deeply can be a potent discussion dynamic.

Buzzing a Group for Saliency

Buzz groups can be used very effectively to follow a large group conversation, in which case real thought must go into structuring the questions that are to be "buzzed." The leader should be reminded also that the dividing of the groups should be done as quickly and easily as possible. The questions may be the same for all the groups, or they may follow a split into whatever areas of differentiation have been planned. They should, however, enhance or sharpen the areas of personal as well as group relevance and identity. For example, if the topic is Adult and Teen-Age Relations, questions to be considered should directly tease out most recent, firsthand experiences with a teen-ager, or an adult, as the case may be.

Group Conversation to Set Up Role Play

For the leader who is trained in role playing and can see applicable incidents to play out for elucidation or for psycho- or sociodramatic impact,[1] group conversation is a particularly fertile source for this kind of material. Here, the experience to be reenacted, with the full potential and range of role playing, is oftentimes the more dramatic and meaningful because it arises in the context of the group's sharing and situation.

The group conversation leader need not be the one to stage the role playing. Often it would be well for the two functions to be lodged in different persons, especially if both are sensitive to group phenomena and to each other's leadership style.

Perhaps for those new to the method, it would be better for the role playing to follow the completion of the group conversation phase. It may not be easy for the novice to keep hold of the mood or direction of the group conversation if the role playing interrupts the general flow of the group conversation, though, by and large, both processes operate on the dimensions of the emotions. As one familiar with the dynamics and procedures of role playing is aware, the closer to the evaluation of the experience the reenactment can come, the greater the psychological impact. However, because the incident is the emotional property of the group, it can be used with effect at any time in the context of the group. Hence, until the group conversation leader develops confidence and competency with his tool, it may be well to let it come as a separate event in the program.

The experienced leader of role playing will see that its use in the context discussed is especially relevant in problems of social or self-inquiry and understanding. Where the group is small and is an ongoing one, it is very often effective to play out the incident as it is offered, in any or all of the ramifications that may ensue in role playing. This is especially true in a psychodramatic situation. The trained group conversation leader can then pick up again and move on through to the next step in the development of the session.

Very often we have found that the playing out of a highly relevant experience becomes the moving and impactful climax of a meeting. It becomes, that is, the dramatic ending of the group conversation session. The sensitive leader will know when this happens and will be guided by the response of the group. Whither the group moves from this point depends on its resources, needs, and maturity as a group, and the awareness, imagination, and creativity of its leaders.

In a measure, this attests to the flexibility of group conversation as a social instrument. It also points to the potency of well-used group resources when leader and participants feel secure and trustful to invest themselves fully and freely in the group. The fullness of the moment can be translated into many kinds of assets on which can be built other dimensions of growth, as an individual, as a group, a community, a people.

Sensitivity Training for Group Growth

Human nature is such a curious complexity and paradox that this kind of fulfillment, this kind of knowing and sensitivity can come from many conditions. Sometimes, indeed, it develops out of a diametrically opposite kind of group situation. From a group climate, for example, in which the participants are so threatened, they feel they must work out their problems and relationships, if they are to survive as a group or as individual personalities. It may be helpful to look at the following example of a situation which is in contrast to the supportive climate of group conversation.

Sensitivity training groups in the Lewinian tradition [2] are oftentimes set up to help participants get to a deeper level of awareness and understanding of personal and social dynamics. Many of the conventional supports, props, and conditions that are consciously or unconsciously built into most group situations, are removed in such training groups. Such supports may include a leadership pre-selected by disposition, interest, status; a group purpose and directedness although frequently inadequately clarified or communicated; a structuring, either well defined or informal; and a predisposition, either by habit or lack of sophistication, to certain kinds of thought and action patterns as a group.

When these supports are removed from a group, the tensions and pressures in looking for a resolution or for more accustomed patterns of group behavior and functioning can be so strong and the frustration so great, that a sensitivity to the need to answer many real needs, which so often are not fulfilled in groups, can be developed. In such stress learning of an impactful dimension can come. This kind of training often requires time and leadership skill of a high order which may not be readily available to many groups. When a group has access, and is exposed, to these resources and training, the experience can indeed be a potent one.

Group conversation, on the other hand, employs resources which are generally available to every group and which are forthcoming if the proper climate is developed. It tries to bring a group quickly to the feeling of trust and security that can make for a relaxed atmosphere so that the spirit can feel free and break through to the deeper levels from which insight can come.

Spontaneity is of the essence, and a well-conducted session can be a moving and profound experience. This seeming paradox implies a delicate balance of trust and expectation. It requires that the leader not only be open to all the magic that can be touched off in a group, but that he be alert to catch the sparks that can set it off. It means that he must be able to convey this faith and sense of ease to the group. He must be on the *qui vive* to contain the exuberance of energies which derive from the recall and interchange of life-renewing memories, but only enough to provide the focus necessary to make the sharing an integrated and integrating experience.

Cultural Democracy, an American Ideal

To encounter again with other human hearts these precious bits of private and social lore is to celebrate their reality and meaningfulness, and the event can be a source of much refreshment and joy upon which to build new learning and growth. When people of culturally mixed beginnings have been encouraged in an atmosphere of acceptance and fun to speak of experiences from their backgrounds, we have found them to do so readily—almost with a sense of urgency. The customs which they share from the old country or down South, or the lower East Side, are seen in their relation to one another as contributions toward a richer American culture.

This process which involves a give-and-take of the best of our traditions and values is *cultural democracy*.

The true democratic concept stems from the deep psychological layers of the human spirit which are the source of these traditions and values. The creative response to life of the Negro as may be seen in the spontaneity and emotional depth of his music, his spirit of endurance maintained through much of his tragic history and circumstance, are values which sustain us all. The family-centered holidays, so important for child development, that are in the tradition of the Jew, the way the Quaker arrives at "the sense of the meeting" without the divisiveness of voting, the "spice and gaiety of life" expressed in the colorful celebrations of the Italian, are only a few of the significant threads in our culture which give emotional content to the American concept of democracy.

Group conversation makes use of these valuable threads that they may be seen in their relationship to the goal that all can give wholeheartedly to the "basic and never-ending drives within our culture to lift itself, to be dissatisfied with its limitations." Such a goal imposes a responsibility, a challenge; it implies an opportunity, indeed an authority. Only in trying to understand and accept our personal involvement in our pluralism and in striving to play our role in the development of our culture and the betterment of humanity can we come to know what is uniquely American in our diversity. Only as we can each fully and freely experience our identity as a person, as a people, as a unity under God can we look toward that one world for which we pray.

NOTES FOR CHAPTER 6

1. Alan F. Klein, *How to Use Role Playing Effectively* (New York: Association Press, 1959).
2. Kurt Lewin, *Resolving Social Conflicts* (New York: Harper & Brothers, 1959); and
   Malcolm and Hulda Knowles, *Introduction to Group Dynamics* (New York: Association Press, 1959).

BIBLIOGRAPHY FOR LEADERS

Abrams, Charles, *Forbidden Neighbors* (New York: Harper & Brothers, 1955). A study of prejudice in housing in the United States, with a suggested program for individual and governmental action.

Adorno, T. W., and others, *The Authoritarian Personality* (New York: Harper & Brothers, 1950). A study of the personality traits of people who are especially susceptible to antidemocratic propaganda. It suggests that those who show the greatest susceptibility to fascist propaganda have many such traits in common.

Adult Education Association of the U.S.A., *How to Use Role Playing*, Leadership Pamphet No. 6 (743 N. Wabash Ave., Chicago, Ill., 1956).

Allport, Gordon W., *The Nature of Prejudice* (New York: Doubleday Anchor Book, paperback, 1958). A comprehensive and penetrating study of the origin and nature of prejudice.

American Friends Service Committee, *Race and Conscience in America* (Norman, Okla.: University of Oklahoma Press, pamphlet, 1959). Prepared by a working party of fourteen, this study of the impact of segregation on every American proclaims the authors' deep belief in the relevance of religious conviction and moral standards to these issues.

———, *Days of Discovery* (20 S. 12th St., Philadelphia 7, Pa., 1960). A series of short pamphlets on seasons and holidays with suggestions for teachers and leaders.

Baruch, Dorothy, *Glass House of Prejudice* (New York: William Morrow and Co., Inc., 1946). A study of the causes and results of prejudice against minority groups in the United States, including a section on "Cures for Prejudice" and a series of questions to test one's own prejudices.

Berthold, Fred, ed., *Basic Sources of the Judeo-Christian Tradition* (Englewood Cliffs, N.J.: Prentice-Hall, Inc., 1962). Selections drawn from original sources in Catholic, Protestant, and Jewish literature.

Bigelow, Karl W., Co-ordinator, Lectures at Conference on Education, *Problems of Special Cultural Groups* (New York: Bureau of Publications, Teachers College, Columbia University, 1951). Cultural diversity is here presented on a world basis by lecturers from several countries.

Borland, Hal, *An American Year* (New York: Simon and Schuster, Inc., 1946). A reflective journal, inspiringly written, describing changes in seasons in the American countryside.

Botkin, B. H., *The Pocket Treasury of American Folklore* (New York: Pocket Books, Inc., 1950). The cream of American folklore, tall tales, ballads, anecdotes, as gathered by an authority on the subject, who says, "If you understand a people's folklore, you understand the people."

Bossard, James H. S., and Boll, Eleanor S., *Ritual in Family Living* (Philadelphia: University of Pennsylvania Press, 1949). A survey of family rituals of three generations shows, according to these authors, that the growing lack of the ceremonial in American life, which so many people mistake for an indication of democracy, may be only cheap tawdriness.

Clark, Kenneth B., *Prejudice and Your Child* (Boston: Beacon Press, 1955). Based on psychological case studies, this authoritative work shows the effects on the personality patterns of both white and Negro children of the societal pressures toward racial awareness, that is, the fundamental moral conflict in the white and the feeling of inferiority in the Negro child.

Collier, John, *Indians of the Americas* (New York: Mentor Books, New American Library, paperbacks, 1959). The author invites us to consider the way of the American Indians, for he sees in their way of life the hope and the fate of mankind.

Council on World Tensions, *Restless Nations: A Study of World Tensions and Development* (New York: Dodd, Mead & Co., 1962). A collection of addresses given at the Oxford Conference on Tensions in Development devoted to establishing workable partnerships between countries in various stages of development.

Dabbs, James McBride, *The Southern Heritage* (New York: Alfred A. Knopf, Inc., 1959). Although this book is considered a classic statement of the enlightened Southern view of race relations, the eloquence and power come from the author's success in seeing all sides of the issue.

Dexter, Harriet, *What's Right with Race Relations* (New York: Harper & Brothers, 1958). Here is the first nationwide account of the hopeful developments in race relations in the last few years.

Douglas, Paul, *The Group Workshop Way in the Church* (New York: Association Press, 1956). An invaluable presentation of the workshop way of training leaders for work in religious institutions.

DuBois, Rachel Davis, *Build Together Americans* (New

York: Hinds, Hayden & Eldredge, 1945). A report of the fifteen secondary schools in one metropolitan area which co-operated in dramatizing the contributions of various groups in American life. These assembly programs, plus a sampling of CBS' radio program "Americans All, Immigrants All" (material for which was supplied by the author), are here available for use in schools.

——, *Get Together Americans* (New York: Harper & Brothers, 1943).

——, *Neighbors in Action* (New York: Harper & Brothers, 1950). A detailed report of how the home and school working together under the PTA, changed the atmosphere of a whole neighborhood by using the method of group conversation.

Duncan, Ethel M., *Democracy's Children* (New York: Hinds, Hayden & Eldredge, 1945). A fifth-grade teacher reports on classroom and assembly seasonal and intergroup programs worked out with her pupils.

Eisenstein, Ira, *Judaism Under Freedom* (New York: The Reconstruction Press, 1958). The author's many years of study of the role of the Jew in American life makes this an invaluable book for both Jew and non-Jew.

Fahs, Sophia L., *Today's Children and Yesterday's Heritage,* A Philosophy of Creative Religions' Development (Boston: Beacon Press, 1952). An appealing and useful book about children and their religious development. Nonsectarian in approach, it stresses the role of the parent and teacher in helping the child to develop his own beliefs about himself and the nature of the universe.

Fromm, Erich, *The Sane Society* (New York: Rinehart & Co., Inc., 1955).

Freud, Sigmund, *The Problems of Anxiety* (New York: W. W. Norton & Co., Inc., 1936).

Gaer, Joseph, *Holidays Around the World* (Boston: Little,

Brown and Co., 1953). Principal Chinese, Hindu, Jewish, Christian, Moslem, and other holidays.

Gaster, Theodor Herzl, *Passover, Its History and Traditions* (New York: Abelard-Schuman, Ltd., 1949).

——, *Purim and Hanukkah in Custom and Tradition* (New York: Abelard-Schuman, Ltd., 1950). The author has gathered information on these two Jewish home and synagogue festivals which, with his own theories, give a special message to both Jew and non-Jew that freedom comes not only from opposing tyranny from without, but equally from overcoming complacency from within.

Gibran, Kahlil, *The Prophet* (New York: Alfred A. Knopf, Inc., 1923). Contains inspiring thoughts on the problems of life; may be of value in the endings of group conversations.

Gordon, Thomas, *Group Centered Leadership* (Boston: Houghton Mifflin Co., 1955). Group centered leadership focuses on ways of relating the creative power in groups.

Hendry, Charles E., *The Role of Groups in World Reconstruction* (New York: Whiteside, Inc., 1952). Leaders in a variety of private, civic, educational organizations from sixty-eight countries analyze the part voluntary groups have played in their countries in developing international understanding. The summary of their responses is not only provocative reading, but helpful as a program guide to groups concerned about international affairs, the work of the United Nations, and the development of understanding of American foreign policy.

Hutchinson, Ruth, and Adams, Ruth, *Everyday's a Holiday* (New York: Harper & Brothers, 1951). A daily calendar of holidays around the world.

Jersild, Arthur T., *In Search of Self* (New York: Bureau of

Publications, Teachers College, Columbia University, 1952). An exploration of the role of the school in promoting self-understanding.

Jung, C. G., *The Undiscovered Self* (New York: Mentor Books, New American Library, 1958). Jung relies on the individual, on his need and capacity to know himself, as the only effective means of combating man's present growing submergence in the mass, whether this be exemplified by submission to the collective state, adherence to religious needs, or the leveling process of scientific, statistical averages. Brief and eminently readable.

Lee, Robert, ed., *Cities and Churches* (Philadelphia: The Westminster Press, 1962). Readings on the urban churches. A collection of articles on the state of the church in urban areas.

Li, Mew-soong and DuBois, Rachel Davis, *Know Your Neighbors* (New York: Workshop for Cultural Democracy, 1955). A new approach in the field of intergroup relations.

Linton, Ralph and Adelin, *Halloween Through Twenty Centuries* (New York: Abelard-Schuman, Ltd., 1950). A treasury of Halloween folklore both religious and magical, delightfully told.

——, *We Gather Together: The Story of Thanksgiving* (New York: Abelard-Schuman, Ltd., 1949). The historical events, traditions, folklore, and songs of this most American of holidays are interestingly told.

Lipman, Eugene, and Vospan, Albert, eds., *A Tale of Ten Cities: The Triple Ghetto in American Religious Life* (New York: Union of American Hebrew Congregations, 1962). General reporting on Christian-Jewish relations and religious tensions, in a cross section of American cities. Lack of index to the names of persons, organizations, or communities is a major weakness.

Masuoka, J., Valien, P., eds., *Race Relations: Problem and Theory* (Chapel Hill, N.C., University of North Carolina Press, 1961). Nineteen social scientists look at various aspects of race relations in a symposium derived from seminars in honor of the late Robert Ezra Park.

Mead, Margaret, *Cultural Patterns and Technical Change* (New York: UNESCO, 1955; reprinted in Mentor paperback, New American Library, 1955). A survey of the impact of technological change on cultural patterns and interfaith understanding.

Miles, Matthew, *Learning to Work in Groups* (New York: Columbia University Press, 1959). A book addressed to the practitioner in the school and in other institutions who seeks to improve his own work. An "attempt to bring together what is now known about the practical problem of helping people learn better group behavior."

Marrow, Alfred J., *Changing Patterns of Prejudice: A New Look at Today's Racial, Religious and Cultural Tensions* (Philadelphia and New York: Chilton Co., 1962). A readable account of intergroup relations problems in New York City, with implications for the national picture by the former Commissioner of Intergroup Relations of that city.

Miller, Haskell M., *Barriers and Bridges to Brotherhood* (New York: Abingdon Press, 1962). A discussion of intergroup problems caused by prejudice, discrimination, and the struggle for power; designed for lay groups.

Monks, James L., *Great Catholic Festivals* (New York: Abelard-Schuman, Ltd., 1951). An interesting account of the origin and spiritual significance of six important Catholic festivals. The book also relates some of the colorful popular customs practiced in these days by people in different countries.

Murphy, Gardner, *Human Potentialities* (New York: Basic

Books, Inc., 1958). One of America's foremost psychologists dramatically shows us how we can, by our free choices, control not only our own destinies, but those of the countless generations to come.

National Association of Intergroup Relations, *The Journal of Intergroup Relations*, a Quarterly (426 W. 58th St., New York 19, N.Y.), their own publication. This journal is concerned with advancing intergroup relations knowledge and skills and furthering acceptance of the goals and principles of intergroup relations work.

Peattie, Donald Culross, *Almanac for Moderns* (New York: G. P. Putnam's Sons, 1935). This book, with a page for each day of the year, gives one a profound sense of unity of all life, including man.

Progoff, Ira, *Depth Psychology and Modern Man* (New York: The Julian Press, Inc., 1959). This book provides an understanding of the principles of experience that underlie faith and a knowledge of practical methods by which an encounter with the meaning of life is possible.

Raab, Earl, and Lipset, Seymour M., *Prejudice and Society*, pamphlet (Anti-Defamation League of B'nai B'rith, 515 Madison Avenue, New York 22, N.Y., 1959). The authors pose the thesis that it is the prejudiced community which is most responsible for widespread prejudiced behavior.

Schauss, Hayyim, *The Jewish Festivals* (Cincinnati: Union of American Hebrew Congregations, 1938). Gives the historical and ceremonial significance of the Jewish festivals and fast days.

Seidenspinner, Clarence, *Great Protestant Festivals* (New York: Abelard-Schuman, Ltd., 1952). The various festivals and services of Protestant churches, from the beginning of the parish year in September to the next summer's close.

Spicer, Dorothy Gladys, *The Book of Festivals* (New York:

The Woman's Press, 1937). Festivals around the year, selected on the basis of nationality, from the Albanians to the Yugoslavs, and showing their commonalities. Most important for leaders of group conversations. Out of print, but should be found in public libraries.

Srole, Leo, Langner, Thomas, and others, *Mental Health in the Metropolis: the Midtown Manhattan Study* (New York: McGraw-Hill Book Co., Inc., 1962). The first volume in the Midtown Manhattan Project which is investigating the interrelationships of psychiatric disorders with sociocultural environment and the stresses of modern living.

Steinberg, Milton, *Basic Judaism* (New York: Harcourt, Brace and Co., 1947). A book about the Jewish religion, its ideals, beliefs, and practices—written for both Jew and non-Jew.

Sykes, John, *The Quakers* (Philadelphia: J. B. Lippincott Co., 1959). This fresh study of the Friends, their history, and their place in the modern world, explains what Quakers basically stand for and why that stand is important.

UNESCO, *What Is Race? Evidence from Scientists* (Paris: Department of Mass Communication, UNESCO, 1952). A summary of the thinking of scientists from all over the world on the nature and problem of race.

van der Post, Laurens, *The Dark Eye in Africa* (New York: William Morrow and Co., Inc., 1955). Of the many white people writing about Africa, van der Post is, no doubt, one of the most sensitive to the feelings of the Africans. His central thesis is that Europeans reject the natural in themselves. This becomes projected on the Negro and turns into fear and hatred. One chapter gives his views on this attitude as applied to the American race problem.

Von Grunebaum, G. E., *Muhammadan Festivals* (New

York: Abelard-Schuman, Ltd., 1951). The drama and beauty of Islam celebrations and ceremonies from their origins to the present day, and how these festivals reflect the many cultural streams that have merged and shaped Islamic civilizations.

Watts, Alan W., *Easter: Its Story and Meaning* (New York: Abelard-Schuman, Ltd., 1950). A beautifully written book in which the author shows that the central theme of Easter—that of death and rebirth—is one that runs in various forms through all cultures. Some of the many folk practices surrounding Easter are also described and explained.

Williams, Robin, *The Reduction of Intergroup Tensions* (Social Science Research Council, 1947). A survey of research on problems of ethnic, racial, and religious group relations prepared under the direction of the New York Committee on Techniques for Reducing Group Hostility.

Wolfram, Eberhard, *Chinese Festivals* (New York: Abelard-Schuman, Ltd., 1951). A rather comprehensive treatment of the important festivals that have sprung from the religio-philosophical patterns of Buddhist, Confucianist, and Taoist practices and that have been woven into the fabric of Chinese life. It shows that some of the same sources that have inspired their celebration have contributed to our own festivals.